The Wealth Equation

Building Financial Freedom Through Skills, Strategy, and Smart Decisions

by Abdul F Abdallah

Disclaimer

"The information contained in this book is intended solely for educational purposes and should not be construed as financial, legal, tax, or investment advice. Readers should consult qualified professionals before making financial decisions."

Dedication

This book is dedicated to every individual who believes that their financial future can be transformed through learning, discipline, perseverance, and purposeful action.

To my family, whose love, encouragement, and sacrifices have inspired my journey.

To my teachers, mentors, colleagues, and students, who continually remind me that knowledge is life's greatest investment.

To entrepreneurs, professionals, business leaders, policymakers, and lifelong learners around the world who strive not merely to earn wealth but to create value, build opportunities, and leave a legacy.

Above all, I dedicate this work to Almighty God, whose wisdom, grace, and guidance make all achievements possible

Foreword

Financial freedom has long been one of humanity's greatest aspirations. Across cultures and generations, people have searched for reliable principles that lead not merely to financial survival but to lasting prosperity. Yet despite the abundance of financial advice available today, many continue to struggle because wealth is often misunderstood. It is commonly perceived as a destination measured solely by income or possessions rather than a lifelong process shaped by knowledge, character, discipline, and purposeful action.

The Wealth Equation offers a refreshing and comprehensive perspective on wealth creation. Rather than focusing exclusively on investing or entrepreneurship, Dr. Abdallah presents a holistic framework that integrates financial literacy, personal development, leadership, technology, innovation, and purposeful living into a practical roadmap for financial success. This foreword reflects the publication-ready version developed in the supplementary suggestions.

One of the strengths of this book is its recognition that wealth creation begins long before money enters a bank account. It begins with mindset. Our beliefs influence our decisions, our decisions determine our habits, and our habits ultimately shape our financial future.

Equally important is the author's emphasis on continuous learning and adaptability. In an age characterized by artificial intelligence, digital transformation, and rapidly changing labor markets, traditional approaches to career development and wealth accumulation are no longer sufficient. Success now belongs to those who embrace innovation, cultivate valuable skills, build meaningful relationships, and remain committed to lifelong learning.

Whether you are a student beginning your financial journey, an entrepreneur building a business, a professional seeking career advancement, or an investor pursuing long-term financial independence, this book provides practical guidance grounded in timeless principles.

May this book inspire you to think differently, act intentionally, and build a legacy that extends far beyond financial success.

Acknowledgements

The completion of this book represents the collective encouragement, wisdom, and support of many individuals and institutions.

I express my deepest gratitude to my family, whose unwavering love, patience, and encouragement have sustained me throughout the writing process.

I am sincerely grateful to my colleagues, mentors, students, and professional associates whose insights, experiences, and constructive discussions have enriched my understanding of leadership, economics, finance, organizational development, and innovation.

My appreciation extends to scholars, researchers, economists, financial practitioners, entrepreneurs, and thought leaders whose published works have contributed to the development of the ideas presented in this book.

Finally, I offer my deepest gratitude to Almighty God for granting me the wisdom, strength, health, and opportunity to complete this work. May this book inspire readers to pursue financial freedom with integrity, wisdom, and purpose.

About the Author

Dr. Abdul Faili Abdallah is an international scholar, banker, economist, leadership expert, educator, and author with extensive professional experience spanning commercial banking, higher education, organizational leadership, business strategy, risk management, human resource development, and financial services.

He has served in senior leadership, academic, and banking positions across multiple institutions and has dedicated his career to helping individuals and organizations improve performance through strategic leadership, financial literacy, innovation, and continuous learning.

Dr. Abdallah holds advanced academic qualifications in economics, management, business administration, organizational leadership, and data sciences. His research and professional interests include financial resilience, artificial intelligence, strategic leadership, organizational agility, banking innovation, economic development, and wealth creation.

Through his teaching, research, consulting, and writing, he seeks to bridge the gap between academic knowledge and practical application, empowering readers to build sustainable wealth and create a legacy.

How to Use This Book

This book is organized as a progressive learning journey.

Each chapter builds upon the previous one and concludes with practical learning tools designed to reinforce understanding and encourage immediate application.

For maximum benefit:

- Read one chapter at a time.
- Reflect on the chapter quotation.
- Complete the reflection questions.
- Implement the recommended action steps.
- Record your progress using the Personal Wealth Toolkit.
- Review your financial goals regularly.
- Revisit the book annually as your financial journey evolves.

Remember:

- Knowledge informs decisions.
- Decisions shape habits.
- Habits determine destiny.

The Wealth Equation Framework

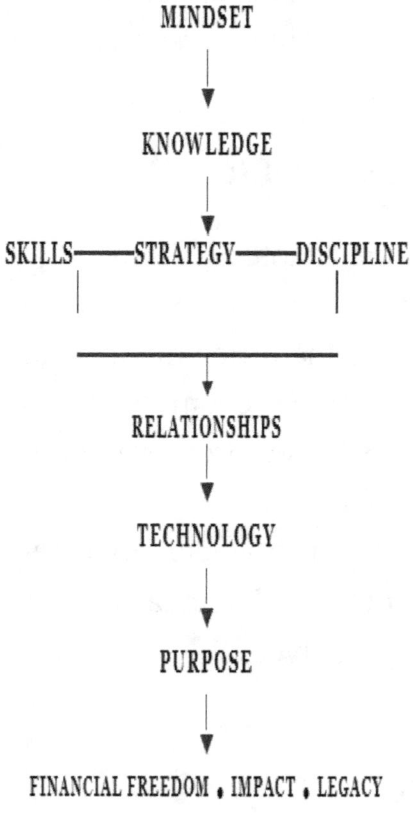

The Wealth Equation (Core Principle)

Wealth = Mindset × Skills × Strategy × Discipline × Relationships × Technology × Purpose

This framework reflects the central theme of the book and aligns with the companion resources and closing message developed in the supporting documents.

Financial freedom is achieved when these elements work together consistently. This equation reminds us that wealth is not determined by income alone—it is built through continuous learning, disciplined execution, strategic investing, meaningful relationships, and a commitment to creating value for others.

Contents

Preface

Welcome to "The Wealth Equation," a journey not just into the mechanics of money, but into the very essence of what it means to create lasting financial freedom. If you have ever felt overwhelmed by the flood of advice, the endless promises of quick wins, or the confusion between wealth and mere accumulation, this book is designed to serve as your trusted compass. It is an invitation to step beyond the noise and chaos of fleeting financial trends and step into a world where wealth is understood, cultivated, and perpetuated with clarity, purpose, and wisdom.

The landscape of wealth creation today is more complex and more dynamic than it has ever been. The stories we grew up hearing—of hard work leading inevitably to prosperity, or of saving every penny to secure a stable future—while still holding fundamental truths, are no longer sufficient on their own. In an era marked by rapid technological evolution, shifting economic paradigms, and unprecedented access to information and tools, the journey toward financial freedom demands more than traditional thinking. It demands a synthesis of mindset transformation, skill acquisition, strategic planning, and a deliberate embrace of innovation. This is why I embarked on writing this book—to provide a roadmap that is as comprehensive as it is practical, as inspiring as it is actionable.

From the very first pages, you will encounter a paradigm shift. We begin by unpacking the psychology of money—a realm too often neglected but crucial. Before wealth can be built, we must understand the invisible forces within our minds that shape our relationship with money: our fears, biases, beliefs, and the deep-seated narratives that either propel us forward or hold us back. Recognizing and reshaping these internal stories is the foundation upon which everything else is constructed. Without this mindset evolution, no amount of skill or strategy can truly effectuate lasting change.

But mindset alone is insufficient. Wealth is ultimately the product of concrete actions informed by knowledge and punctuated by leadership and purposeful entrepreneurship. These chapters invite you to explore the indispensable skill sets that transform potential into reality. Whether it's advancing your career with intention, developing leadership that inspires and empowers, or embracing entrepreneurship as a vehicle for innovation and wealth creation, each path is explored with nuance and insight. This progression from internal readiness to external mastery ensures that you are not merely dreaming but actively building.

At the heart of this book is the recognition that wealth is not a solitary pursuit. Human connections, relationships, and the discipline to sustain growth are the catalysts that amplify opportunity and resilience. By weaving stories and strategies around the cultivation of human capital, the narrative highlights how wealth extends far beyond financial statements—it is about community, trust, and shared vision. Discipline emerges as the unseen force behind every successful endeavor, and its subtle power is brought to life through practical frameworks designed to develop habits that support sustained progress.

Emerging technologies, particularly artificial intelligence, are reshaping every aspect of life, including how we approach wealth. Far from being abstract concepts reserved for tech elites, AI and digital tools are now accessible partners in strategic decision-making and financial management. This book demystifies these technologies and illuminates their transformative potential. You will see how harnessing AI an advantage is not just but swiftly becoming a necessity for anyone serious about staying ahead in the wealth-building game.

What sets "The Wealth Equation" apart is the seamless integration of these domains—mindset, skills, strategy, relationships, and technology—into a cohesive framework. Each chapter builds upon the last, creating a fabric of understanding that invites you to think holistically about your financial future. No sudden shortcuts or empty promises, but a deeply considered, step-by-step approach tailored to the realities and opportunities of our time.

Perhaps most importantly, this book champions the idea that true wealth is rooted in purpose and legacy. Financial freedom is far more meaningful when aligned with values that transcend the individual and ripple outward, impacting families, communities, and generations to come. It is this vision of wealth as a living, ethical force—grounded in wisdom, character, and discipline—that I am passionate about sharing with you. In doing so, I hope to inspire not only personal transformation but a broader movement toward responsible and sustaining prosperity.

Throughout these pages, you will encounter stories, real-world examples, and reflective questions designed to engage your mind and spirit. This is not a passive read; it is a call to active participation in your own journey toward freedom and fulfillment. The chapters vary in tone and length, mirroring the ebbs and flows of a real expedition, keeping you alert, motivated, and curious. Whether you are a dreamer with an inspired vision or a doer ready to roll up your sleeves, this book offers tools, insights, and encouragement tailored to your unique path.

I invite you to begin with an open heart and an eager mind. The road ahead may challenge what you thought you knew, but it will reward your courage with the gift of empowerment and clarity. Building wealth is not an elusive mystery reserved for a chosen few; it is an equation—one that you hold the variables to solve. As you turn these pages, you may find not only knowledge but inspiration; not only strategy but wisdom; and ultimately, not just financial freedom but a life rich in purpose, growth, and legacy.

Welcome to "The Wealth Equation." Your journey toward lasting prosperity starts now.

Chapter 1:
The Psychology of Wealth

"Whether you think you can, or you think you can't—you're right." — Henry Ford

Key Takeaways

- Wealth creation begins with developing the right mindset.
- Your beliefs about money influence every financial decision you make.
- Limiting beliefs can prevent financial growth and must be challenged.
- A growth mindset creates opportunities where others see obstacles.
- Emotional intelligence improves financial decision-making.
- Financial success starts with changing your thinking before changing your income.
- Purpose and resilience are essential ingredients of lasting wealth.

Understanding Money Mindsets

Money, in its simplest form, is a tool—a means of exchange, a store of value, a measure of worth. Yet, for all its apparent simplicity, the concept of money has taken on complex psychological, emotional, and even spiritual dimensions in human experience. These underlying mental frameworks and attitudes toward money, often referred to as money mindsets, shape not only how we earn, save, and spend but fundamentally influence the trajectory of our financial lives. Understanding money mindsets is therefore crucial, for it is here that the seeds of financial empowerment or entrapment are sown. The way we relate to money, often shaped in early childhood and reinforced by cultural narratives, family conditioning, social environment, and individual life experiences, forms a prism through which every financial decision is filtered. It is this unseen internal architecture—the collection of beliefs, fears, aspirations, and habits—that determines whether money becomes a source of freedom or a source of anxiety.

At the heart of this examination lies the recognition that money mindsets are rarely neutral; they are charged with emotion and loaded with meaning. Many people carry limiting beliefs about wealth that quietly sabotage their best intentions. These beliefs might include ideas such as "money is the root of all evil," a distorted interpretation of a biblical phrase that has stigmatized wealth accumulation and cast financial success as morally questionable. Others might believe "I don't deserve to be wealthy," or "rich people are greedy and dishonest," patterns of thinking that foster self-sabotage and prevent individuals from pursuing or accepting prosperity. These narratives often go unchallenged, leading people to unconsciously restrict the flow of money in their lives by avoiding risks, undervaluing their skills, or failing to invest in their growth. The result is a cyclical pattern where financial stress feeds negative mindsets, and these mindsets in turn perpetuate financial stress.

On the opposite end of the spectrum are empowering money mindsets, those that view wealth creation as a positive, ethical, and necessary pursuit that enables individuals to improve not only their own lives but also the lives of those around them. This frame reframes money from being either a source of fear or guilt to being a force for good, a catalyst for opportunity, growth, and contribution. Individuals harboring such mindsets tend to approach money with curiosity and confidence rather than anxiety and resistance. They perceive challenges as opportunities for learning and view failures as temporary setbacks rather than definitive judgments of worth. They understand the fundamental principle that financial freedom is crafted through intention, discipline, and aligned actions, not luck or chance. This mindset fuels habits such as consistent saving, strategic spending, ongoing education, and entrepreneurial risk-taking—behaviors that cumulatively build financial resilience and wealth.

Yet, it is important to recognize that money mindsets rarely exist in pure forms; instead, they weave a complex tapestry, often changing and evolving with circumstances and consciousness. For many, ambivalence or conflicting messages about money create internal tension that manifests in inconsistent financial behavior. For example, someone may earn well and save diligently, yet feel extreme guilt spending on themselves, depriving their lifestyle of joy. Another might dream of entrepreneurship but be overwhelmed by fear of failure, hesitating to take the leap that could unlock higher income potential. These internal conflicts, though subtle, can erode progress and diminish the sense of agency crucial to financial success. Awareness of these psychological dynamics is the first step toward transformation. By bringing these subconscious beliefs and emotions to light, individuals can begin to question their validity, disentangle false narratives, and consciously cultivate more constructive attitudes toward money.

Delving deeper, it becomes clear that money is not merely an external resource but a mirror reflecting one's self-worth and identity. A core barrier to wealth creation is often an unconscious link between money and personal value. If an individual equates their self-worth directly with their net worth, it sets the stage for emotional turmoil tied to financial fluctuations. Conversely, those who develop a stable sense of identity and purpose independent of their bank balance are better equipped to weather financial ups and downs with resilience. This distinction matters; it emphasizes that building a healthy money mindset is not just about mastering financial literacy but about nurturing emotional intelligence and self-awareness. Cultivating self-compassion, recognizing intrinsic value beyond material success, and embracing a growth mindset in the broader life context foster a foundation where financial goals are pursued without fear, shame, or desperation.

Significantly, the cultural context plays a monumental role in shaping an individual's money mindset. Societal norms and values, peer influences, media portrayals, and collective narratives about wealth saturate the environment, influencing perceptions often beneath conscious awareness. In many cultures, discussions about money remain taboo, laden with embarrassment or conflict, which fuels secrecy and misinformation. Others may glorify conspicuous consumption and instant gratification, pushing unrealistic expectations and financial behaviors that are unsustainable. In this psychological ecosystem, one's money mindset is continually reflexive—it absorbs, reacts to, and refines itself through external stimuli. Understanding that one's personal money story is embedded within and influenced by this larger social milieu helps contextualize challenges and prevent internalization of blame when obstacles arise.

Within the framing of wealth creation, emotional factors such as fear and scarcity often exert a disproportionate influence on financial decisions. Fear of not having enough can drive behaviors such as hoarding money, avoiding investments, or resisting career advancement to remain safely within comfort zones. The scarcity mindset—a pervasive feeling that resources are limited and opportunities rare—creates a psychological prison that limits innovation, generosity, and risk appetite. Conversely, the abundance mindset, which views resources as plentiful and opportunities as accessible, encourages proactive exploration, generosity, and strategic risk-taking. The transition from scarcity to abundance mindset is pivotal in shifting financial trajectories. Achieving this shift requires conscious practice, starting with gratitude for current resources, focusing on possibilities rather than obstacles, and reinforcing beliefs that one's efforts will be rewarded through time and learning rather than immediate gratification.

Transforming one's money mindset is not solely an intellectual endeavor but a deeply personal and emotional journey. It requires intentional engagement with one's internal narrative. Reflective exercises such as journaling about past money experiences, identifying recurring limiting thoughts, and analyzing emotional triggers around money can illuminate hidden biases. Equally important are daily practices that reprogram the subconscious mind, including affirmations, visualization of financial goals, and immersing oneself in success stories that break stereotypical molds. Surrounding oneself with mentors, coaches, or communities that embody positive money mindsets reinforces new patterns and provides accountability. Each small mental shift, repeated over time, compounds into a new habit of thinking—one that aligns cognition, emotion, and behavior towards wealth-building.

Understanding the critical relationship between money mindset and financial behavior also sheds light on why traditional financial education often falls short. Most conventional programs focus heavily on mechanics—budgeting, investing, credit scores—but pay insufficient attention to the psychological dimension that underpins those activities. Without addressing the mental and emotional framework, individuals may gain knowledge but fail to translate it into lasting empowerment, as obsolete money scripts continue to drive unconscious choices. Integrating psychology with financial literacy offers a far more effective approach, one that nurtures both knowledge and confidence. This dual focus enables people not only to understand the mechanics of wealth but to embody the attitudes and resilience needed to apply those skills consistently, adapt to change, and persevere through setbacks.

Moreover, it is essential to recognize that money mindset development is not a one-time fix but a lifelong process. Life events, economic changes, career shifts, and personal growth stages naturally require reevaluation and recalibration of beliefs and behaviors related to money. Sustainable wealth creation is therefore dynamic, fluid, and responsive. Each phase of life offers new lessons and opportunities to deepen one's relationship with money. For instance, what drives a young professional's money thinking differs vastly from someone preparing for retirement or transitioning to entrepreneurship. A mature money mindset integrates flexibility with firm values, enabling individuals to navigate diverse financial landscapes while holding onto their core principles of responsibility, integrity, and purpose.

In practice, cultivating a positive money mindset involves embracing discomfort. It means confronting fears about scarcity, overcoming shame or guilt associated with past financial missteps, and challenging deeply ingrained societal narratives. This discomfort is a sign of growth, an indication that old paradigms are being questioned and new pathways forged. Successful wealth creators often describe an evolving internal dialogue—one that moves from self-doubt to self-trust, from hesitation to decisive action, and from reactive scarcity to proactive abundance. This internal transformation manifests externally as better financial decisions, improved relationships with money, and ultimately greater freedom and security.

Another dimension worth considering is the interplay between money mindset and identity beyond the individual level. Family systems, cultural heritage, and generational patterns transmit money beliefs across time. Understanding the legacy of these intergenerational scripts provides insight into behaviors that may seem irrational or unexplainable on the surface. For example, a family culture rooted in poverty may embed narratives of limitation, while inherited wealth may carry expectations or anxieties around stewardship. By bringing these inherited scripts to consciousness, individuals gain the power to redefine their money story, breaking cycles of scarcity or dysfunction and initiating new traditions of abundance and wisdom.

The role of purpose and alignment with values also cannot be overstated in the development of a healthy money mindset. Wealth pursued solely for material gain often leads to dissatisfaction; however, when financial goals are connected to a greater sense of meaning, whether it be supporting family, contributing to community, or enabling creative expression—money transforms from a mere transaction into a vehicle for impact and fulfillment. This purposeful alignment deepens motivation, fortifies discipline, and enriches the experience of financial success, making wealth not just an end but a means to a life well lived.

Importantly, as technology and artificial intelligence redefine economic landscapes, the adaptability of one's money mindset becomes a critical asset. The rapid pace of change demands not only technical skills but psychological agility to embrace uncertainty, innovate, and seize emerging opportunities. A mindset rooted in curiosity, continuous learning, and resilience will navigate disruption with confidence, while fixed or fearful mentalities will struggle. Therefore, cultivating a forward-looking money mindset that balances prudence with openness can become a decisive factor in building and sustaining wealth in the modern world.

In summary, understanding money mindsets invites a profound exploration of self—as emotional beings, as value-driven actors, and as participants in cultural and generational narratives. It challenges readers to step beyond surface financial tactics into the realm of inner transformation. By identifying and dismantling limiting beliefs, embracing empowering attitudes, addressing the emotional and cultural roots of money behavior, and aligning financial goals with purpose, individuals unlock the true potential of wealth creation. This journey is not linear nor easy, but it is deeply rewarding. The mindset acts as the invisible architecture supporting every brick and beam of financial strategy. Without a solid, positive money mindset, even the best plans falter; with it, the possibilities for growth, freedom, and legacy become truly expansive. Ultimately, this understanding lays the cornerstone for all subsequent wealth-building endeavors, inviting readers to embark on a path where money serves as a powerful companion rather than a source of conflict path illuminated by clarity, confidence, and conscious choice

Overcoming Limiting Beliefs

Across the vast, intricate landscape of wealth creation, the invisible walls we erect within our own minds often impose the greatest constraints on our journey to financial freedom. These walls, formed by deep-seated limiting beliefs, are powerful psychological barriers that subtly yet profoundly influence how we perceive money, opportunity, and our own potential to generate wealth. To understand and dismantle these mental constraints is not merely an intellectual exercise but a foundational step toward transforming one's financial trajectory. These beliefs, often cloaked in assumptions, fears, and cultural narratives, shape every decision and reaction related to money, dictating whether a person seizes an opportunity or shrinks back in hesitation, whether they invest in themselves or settle for the status quo. Recognizing the presence and power of these limiting beliefs is the first, vital step toward overcoming them and cultivating a mindset that does not just hope for financial success but actively engineer it.

One of the most common limiting beliefs that many hold is the notion that wealth is inherently a zero-sum game—if someone else gains financially, you must lose. This perception engenders a scarcity mindset, where financial resources and opportunities are viewed as finite and fiercely competitive rather than abundant and collaborative. When entrenched in this belief, individuals may approach wealth creation with suspicion of others' success, fear of taking risks, and a reluctance to innovate or share resources. The scarcity mindset fosters anxiety over money, causing paralysis in decision-making or reckless conservatism that impedes growth. Overcoming this barrier requires a conscious shift toward abundance thinking, which is an acknowledgment that the economy and the possibilities for wealth creation are expansive, and one's success does not preclude that of others. This shift involves rewiring one's cognitive frameworks to see opportunity as boundless, fostering generosity and collaboration, which paradoxically expands one's own access to wealth networks and ideas.

Closely related to the scarcity belief is the pervasive fear that "money is the root of all evil," a deeply ingrained cultural adage that taints money with moral suspicion. This poisonous lie, often absorbed unwittingly from family or societal conditioning, frames the pursuit of wealth as inherently selfish or corrupting. Such a belief creates an emotional conflict where the aspiration to acquire financial security is at odds with moral self-identity, forcing an internal divide that impairs financial decisions or ambition. Individuals trapped in this paradigm may self-sabotage opportunities for wealth, either through procrastination, avoidance of financial responsibility, or unconscious behaviors that limit earnings. Contrarily, reframing this idea reveals that money itself is ethically neutral tool that can amplify both good and ill depending on its steward. Embracing this perspective frees one to pursue wealth to achieve personal autonomy, support loved ones, contribute to social causes, and create lasting legacies that align with one's values and integrity.

Another powerful, yet often unacknowledged limiting belief is the idea that financial success requires extraordinary luck, privilege, or resources far beyond one's reach. This belief can create a victim mentality, where individuals attribute their lack of wealth not to choices or efforts but to external circumstances that seem immutable. Such fatalism dulls initiative and blinds individuals to the inventory of skills, networks, and incremental steps available to them. It also diminishes the practical understanding that wealth-building is a process enriched by perseverance, learning from failures, and iterative progress rather than immediate leaps. Confronting this belief involves cultivating a growth mindset, which insists that abilities and fortunes can be developed through dedication and strategic effort. Real-world success stories reinforce this transformation, illustrating how individuals, often starting with modest means, elevate their economic status by navigating challenges creatively and persistently. In essence, luck favors the prepared mind, and preparation emerges from learned skills and resilient mindsets available to anyone willing to evolve.

Fear of taking risks is another mental block that inhibits wealth generation. Many fears losing what little they have rather than risking uncertainty for the possibility of significant gain. This risk aversion is less about numbers on a balance sheet and more about emotional safety and the avoidance of perceived failure. Drawing comfort from the familiar financial limbo, individuals may resist investing in growth opportunities, education, or entrepreneurial ventures, thereby limiting their income potential and wealth accumulation. The primary method to overcome this hurdle is reframing failure not as a catastrophe but as a necessary and informative component of growth. Re-educating the emotional response to risk, encouraging calculated experimentation, and developing financial literacy to evaluate risks objectively help to neutralize paralyzing fear. Gradually, individuals learn that measured risk-taking is essential for moving beyond subsistence into economies of scale and diversification. This process is most effective when supported by deliberate risk management strategies that combine research, mentorship, incremental steps, and contingency planning.

Embedded in many minds is also the constricting belief that wealth is solely the result of hard labor and that financial success cannot be divorced from relentless toil. This narrative glorifies a workaholic culture and often neglects the critical role of strategic thinking, efficiency, and leveraging assets to generate passive income. It encourages a trade of time for money and undervalues the skills of delegation, automation, and innovative entrepreneurship. The limitation here is an incomplete understanding of what true wealth encompasses —

financial freedom that allows time to be spent on purpose-driven activities rather than perpetual labor. Overcoming this belief mandates a paradigm shift from sheer effort to smart effort, affirming that wealth creation is as much about strategy, innovation, and mindset as it is about work ethics. Financial education plays a crucial role here, teaching how to identify and build multiple streams of income, invest wisely, and capitalize on leverage points that multiply returns beyond direct labor input.

A subtle yet corrosive belief that undermines financial progress is the idea that one is undeserving or incapable of wealth. Rooted often in early experiences of scarcity, familial messaging, or societal stereotypes, this belief triggers imposter syndrome and self-limitation. People burdened by this mindset may feel that wealth is reserved for others with superior intelligence, education, connections, or luck—and thus avoid setting ambitious financial goals or seeking growth opportunities. This self-doubt infiltrates intentions, tainting efforts with hesitation and missed chances. Overcoming this requires deliberate work to build self-esteem, affirm one's intrinsic worthiness of prosperity, and dismantle negative self-talk. Techniques drawn from cognitive behavioral therapy, affirmations, visualization, and surrounding oneself with supportive communities can reinforce a positive financial identity. Recognizing that everyone, regardless of background, has the potential to learn, adapt, and succeed is key to unlocking this psychological lock.

Moreover, emotional attachment to money itself or the absence thereof can create invisible barriers. Some individuals harbor guilt for acquiring wealth thinking it separates them from their community or origins, while others feel anxiety when faced with financial abundance because it challenges their conditioned norms of modesty or frugality. Conversely, some with little financial resources may have a numb detachment from their finances, leading to neglect and poor money management. This emotional misalignment distorts the ability to engage with financial reality objectively, causing either over-restriction or recklessness. Developing emotional intelligence around money involves acknowledging and processing these feelings without judgment, thereby enabling rational and aligned financial decisions. Journaling, mindful reflection, and financial coaching can facilitate this emotional reconciliation, turning money from a source of inner conflict into a resource for empowerment and growth.

To systematically overcome these limiting beliefs, a multi-faceted approach is essential. Awareness serves as the cornerstone—simply identifying these mental roadblocks with honesty and compassion opens the door for change. This might involve reflective journaling where one traces origins of beliefs, or candid conversations with mentors and peers who can offer perspective and challenge irrational narratives. Next, reprogramming these beliefs demands consistent action aligned with new empowering narratives. Setting small, achievable financial goals creates positive feedback loops, reinforcing the belief in one's capacity to influence their wealth trajectory. Education amplifies this process, equipping individuals with the knowledge and skills to navigate financial systems confidently, replacing guesswork and fear with clarity and competence.

Visualization and affirmations are powerful tools to rewire the subconscious mind. By vividly imagining financial success achieved through deliberate action, individuals create emotional connections with desired outcomes, making those futures feel tangible and attainable. Affirmations applied regularly counteract the negative internal dialogue that asserts limitations, slowly replacing it with a language of possibility and strength. Partnering these psychological tools with pragmatic financial habits—budgeting, investing, networking, and continuous learning—builds a comprehensive strategy that addresses both belief and behavior.

Accountability and community involvement further accelerate this transformation. Engaging with like-minded individuals who share growth aspirations creates a supportive ecosystem, where challenges are normalized, successes celebrated, and encouragement abundant. This communal reinforcement breaks isolation that often feeds limiting beliefs while exposing one to diverse perspectives and opportunities. Coaching or masterminding groups can provide structured support, offer tailored guidance and holding individuals accountable to their commitments, which increases resilience and motivation.

Lastly, embracing the inevitable setbacks as integral to the journey nurtures resilience, a critical attribute for long-term wealth creation. Rather than interpreting failures as proof of inability, reframing them as experiments yielding valuable data fosters persistence. Cultivating patience, empathy towards oneself, and a problem-solving orientation transforms obstacles into stepping stones rather than impassable walls. This mental agility is what separates sustainable financial success from ephemeral wins.

Conquering limiting beliefs is not a finite task but a lifelong practice, as new challenges and stages of wealth accumulation bring fresh psychological landscapes to navigate. The richness of this internal work lies in its profound ripple effects—not only enhancing financial outcomes but also enriching personal growth, relationships, and overall well-being. As individuals move beyond their mental constraints, they unlock reservoirs of creativity, courage, and vision that propel them into expanding realms of possibility. They begin to understand that wealth is not an exclusive club guarded by fortune or heritage, but a dynamic equation requiring the right mindset, skills, and strategies, all starting within the mind.

Liberation from limiting beliefs transforms not just individual bank accounts but entire life narratives. It paves the way for wealth to serve as a true tool of freedom to pursue purpose, create impact, and build enduring legacies. By confronting and overcoming these invisible barriers, readers empower themselves to rewrite their wealth stories, turning mental captivity into mental mastery, and opening the gates to a future where financial freedom is not a distant dream but an intentional, lived reality.

Building a Growth-Oriented Financial Mindset

Developing a growth-oriented financial mindset is not merely a wishful notion or a spiritual aspiration; it is a deliberate, purposeful process that demands careful attention to the intricate interplay of thoughts, beliefs, habits, and emotional conditioning relating to money and wealth. At the heart of this transformation lies the ability to adopt an adaptive and opportunity-focused approach—a mindset that is not only welcoming of challenges but thrives on the possibilities that uncertainty and change bring. To build this mindset, one must first confront the mental frameworks and emotional factors that govern how money is perceived and handled. These are often deeply ingrained from early experiences, cultural narratives, societal conditioning, and personal history. For many, the journey to financial freedom—and indeed, to a sustainable and fulfilling wealth equation—starts with facing the limiting beliefs that quietly but powerfully sabotage progress. These beliefs manifest in numerous ways: the conviction that wealth is for the lucky or the privileged, the idea that money is inherently corrupting or evil, the fear of loss that paralyzes investment desires, or the mindset that financial success requires sacrificing happiness and personal values. These pervasive limitations serve as invisible shackles, confining individuals to patterns of scarcity, hesitation, and self-doubt, which block not only the accumulation of wealth but also the enjoyment and purposeful use of it.

To transcend these limiting narratives, one must first acknowledge their existence and trace their roots with fearless honesty. This introspective excavation lays the foundation for change. Awareness is the critical first step because until these beliefs are surfaced and examined, they operate beneath conscious recognition, steering decisions with emotional irrationality rather than strategic intent. As you pull these beliefs into the light of conscious thought, begin to interrogate them rigorously: Are they based on fact or fear? Were they formed in response to specific experiences, or are they handed down generational myths? How do they shape your daily financial decisions, your willingness to take risk, your perception of what is possible? This process, though uncomfortable at times, opens the doorway to freedom. It initiates a mental reset, allowing you to begin reconnecting with desire, possibility, and control rather than anxiety and limitation.

From there, the cultivation of a new financial mindset becomes a matter of nurturing adaptive thinking patterns that embrace learning, resilience, and opportunity. This is the hallmark of a growth-oriented mentality: the fundamental belief that financial intelligence and capability can improve over time with effort, experience, and intention, much like any other skill. It involves replacing scarcity with abundance, fear with curiosity, and resignation with proactive strategy. Rather than viewing obstacles as dead ends, they become puzzles to solve and steppingstones toward new horizons. Every setback transforms into feedback, every challenge an invitation to innovate. This shift demands that you develop emotional agility- the capacity to manage negative emotions like fear, envy, and impatience without being overwhelmed by them—and instead cultivate positive emotions such as hope, gratitude, and confidence, which are scientifically linked to improved decision-making and perseverance.

One effective technique to foster this resilience and opportunity focus is the practice of reframing—actively changing the narrative you tell yourself about financial experiences. For example, instead of interpreting a missed investment opportunity as failure, view it as a lesson learned about timing or market conditions. Instead of beating yourself up for a financial mistake, frame it as an essential moment of growth that sharpens your judgment and builds experience. This habitual reframing retrains your brain to hunt for silver linings and lessons rather than crumble under negative self-talk. Over time, this cognitive restructuring alters neural pathways, making optimism and resourcefulness your default modes of thought, enabling you to stay mentally nimble in an ever-evolving financial landscape.

Another critical dimension to nurturing a growth-oriented financial mindset is envisioning long-term possibilities while staying grounded in actionable short-term goals. Dreaming big about financial freedom, security, and impact creates the motivational fuel necessary for enduring the rigors of wealth-building. However, these dreams must be paired with a realistic acknowledgment of the present moment, your starting point, and the incremental steps required. This balanced perspective prevents overwhelm and fosters sustainable progress. Techniques such as journaling future aspirations, coupled with daily financial check-ins, accountability partnerships, or mentor guidance, can strengthen this dynamic, ensuring that your mindset remains both visionary and practical. This fusion of aspiration and pragmatism sustains momentum and fosters a continuous cycle of growth.

Integral to this mental transformation is cultivating a sense of purpose—ensuring that the pursuit of wealth is not divorced from personal values, passions, or a broader mission. When your money mindset is tied to meaningful goals, be it supporting family, creating community impact, or enabling innovation, wealth transcends mere accumulation and becomes a vehicle for fulfillment. This connection to purpose shifts motivation from short-term gratification to long-term satisfaction, cushioning you against setbacks and keeping you aligned with authentic desires rather than fleeting trends or external validation. Purpose-driven finance creates a compelling why, essential for maintaining discipline and focus on the complex journey of wealth creation.

Practically, building a growth-oriented financial mindset also depends heavily on knowledge acquisition and skill development. The belief that you can learn, adapt, and optimize your financial strategies fosters confidence and reduces anxiety. Continuous learning about budgeting, investing, tax planning, entrepreneurship, and financial psychology expands your toolkit and empowers you to make informed, agile decisions. The excitement of mastering new concepts feeds a positive feedback loop that fuels motivation. Moreover, surrounding yourself with a community of learners, mentors, and like-minded individuals accelerates growth by providing support, accountability, and diverse perspectives. Networking is not merely a transactional activity; it is a mindset built on mutual enrichment and shared opportunity.

Within this growth mindset framework, embracing failure emerges as a vital cultural norm. Instead of fearing mistakes or setbacks, viewing them as essential components of a rich learning tapestry liberates you to innovate and take measured risks. Failure becomes a teacher without judgment, a momentary deviation rather than a permanent verdict. This attitude dissolves the paralysis induced by fear and perfectionism, which are among the most common inhibitors of financial progress. Stories of renowned entrepreneurs and financiers are replete with setbacks that, when reframed, became fuel for subsequent triumphs. By cultivating this stance, your psychological resilience strengthens, and your capacity to recover and iterate in your financial journey grows exponentially.

Emotional intelligence plays a central role in maintaining adaptive financial behavior over time. Awareness and management of impulses, biases, and moods guard against fatigue and discouragement, which can trigger poor decisions like impulsive spending or premature withdrawal from investment opportunities. Mindfulness practices, meditation, and routine reflection about your emotional state in relation to money decisions improve self-regulation. Developing curiosity about the emotional influences on financial behavior enhances self-knowledge and supports a proactive rather than reactive approach. Additionally, cultivating gratitude for existing resources shifts your focus from scarcity to sufficiency, a psychological state that nurtures generosity, patience, and strategic thinking, all of which are conducive to sustainable wealth growth.

Financial literacy is, of course, a cornerstone of this mindset but not merely in the rote acquisition of facts about interest rates or investment vehicles. It must be intertwined with critical thinking and the ability to apply knowledge contextually and creatively. Understanding the broader economic forces at play, such as market cycles, inflation, and technological disruption, enables you to navigate complexity without panic or complacency. This equips you to identify opportunities early and avoid pitfalls that less-informed individuals fall prey to. Integrating analytical rigor with intuition, enhanced through experience, positions you to respond dynamically to shifts rather than react defensively.

Technological advancement, especially in the digital and artificial intelligence realm, offers additional catalysts for a growth-oriented financial mindset. Engaging with technology as an enabler rather than a threat stimulates curiosity and adaptability, key cognitive traits enhancing your ability to innovate and find novel avenues for wealth generation. Using AI-driven financial tools, investment analysis algorithms, and platforms that support entrepreneurial ventures enhances your capacity to scale and optimize your financial activities. This embrace of technology must be embedded within a mindset that welcomes change, learns continuously, and continually scans the horizon for new breakthroughs that could be applied advantageously.

Bridging the personal with the universal, building a growth-oriented financial mindset also calls for a communal perspective—recognizing that wealth exists in ecosystems of relationships, mutual support, and shared values. The old paradigms of wealth as a zero-sum game are increasingly untenable in an interconnected world. Instead, fostering generosity, collaboration, and social capital becomes a strategic and psychological asset. When you view your financial journey as part of a larger narrative involving family, community, and even global impact, your mindset shifts from isolated accumulation to purposeful stewardship. This perspective breeds resilience because it anchors your wealth-building not just in personal gain but in legacy, connection, and contribution.

Changing one's mindset is not a linear process but a layered and iterative transformation. It involves daily choices—what thoughts to nourish, which voices to silence, what habits to form. Repetition, consistent reflection, and intentional practice shape the neural architecture of your financial psychology. Visualization exercises, affirmations, goal setting, and storytelling are powerful techniques that reinforce a positive money narrative, embedding growth orientation deeply into your subconscious. Combined with accountability structures such as coaching or peer groups, these practices cement new neural pathways creating a stable and resilient mental foundation for wealth.

In sum, building a growth-oriented financial mindset is a holistic endeavor weaving together awareness of limiting beliefs, emotional regulation, purpose alignment, continuous learning, resilience to failure, adaptive strategies in the face of technological change, and an ethic of contribution. It requires courage to face ingrained fears and myths, discipline to implement new habits, and vision to see wealth as a dynamic, evolving journey rather than a fixed state. Achieving this mindset does not guarantee wealth overnight, but it unlocks the most potent resource for financial success: your own mental ecosystem capable of creative problem-solving, strategic risk-taking, and enduring commitment. By cultivating this internal architecture, you set yourself on a trajectory where opportunity becomes the default environment, and wealth manifests organically—not as a frantic chase, but as the natural outcome of an empowered and evolving individual.

Chapter 2: Foundations of Financial Literacy

"An investment in knowledge pays the best interest." — Benjamin Franklin

Key Takeaways

- Financial literacy is the foundation of long-term financial success.
- Budgeting gives every dollar a purpose.
- Saving consistently creates financial security.
- An emergency fund protects against unexpected setbacks.
- Compound interest rewards early and disciplined saving.
- Managing debt wisely preserves wealth.
- Financial knowledge increases confidence and reduces costly mistakes.

Budgeting and Saving Strategies

Mastering the art of budgeting and saving is the cornerstone of financial wellness, the indispensable first step toward wealth creation. At its core, budgeting is a thoughtful and deliberate process of mapping income against expenses to create a sustainable rhythm for managing money. It requires not just the organization of dollars and cents but a deep understanding of one's values, priorities, and long-term objectives. Without this clarity, money often flows unchecked and unnoticed, like water slipping through the cracks of a bucket, leaving individuals perpetually stranded on the shores of financial uncertainty. Effective budgeting is a form of self-leadership; it demands discipline and the willingness to confront uncomfortable truths about spending habits and lifestyle choices. Through this process, one gains awareness of financial patterns—both productive and destructive—and can begin to take intentional control over the journey toward saving and investing.

The foundation of good budgeting rests on the accurate and comprehensive recording of all income sources. This is often simpler than people assume, yet it requires vigilance, especially in a world where side gigs, freelance work, and passive income streams increasingly supplement traditional salaries. Recognizing and consolidating every source of money entering your hands creates a clear starting point for managing outgoing expenditures. Income without a plan is like fuel without an engine, incapable of propelling you anywhere meaningfully. Once your income is understood, the critical work of examining expenses begins—tracking where every dollar goes, from recurring bills and essential needs to discretionary spending and occasional indulgences. This exercise of transparent accounting is not designed to induce guilt but to cultivate awareness. Many are surprised to discover how even small, frequent outflows—such as daily coffee purchases or subscriptions that go unused—erode their capacity to save.

Budgeting is not about deprivation; it is about prioritization and making trade-offs aligned with personal values. It is the financial manifestation of one's internal compass. Effective budgeters design their spending around categories that reflect what matters most—whether that's securing a home, investing in education, nurturing relationships, or building a nest egg for the future. By thoughtfully allocating funds in this way, budgeting transforms from a sterile spreadsheet into a living blueprint for purposeful living. One particularly effective approach is the zero-based budget, where every dollar of income is assigned a specific task, from essentials and debts to savings and investments. This technique leaves no room for idle funds and prevents accidental overspending, ensuring that money works constructively toward wealth accumulation rather than dissipating unnoticed.

Saving, the natural twin to budgeting, is the practice of intentionally setting aside portions of income for future use. While it might seem straightforward, saving effectively requires strategic consideration informed by clear goals and an understanding of the various types of savings and their respective functions. Emergency savings, for example, serve as a financial buffer, a protective shield against unexpected shocks such as medical emergencies, job loss, or urgent home repairs. Without this safety net, unforeseen expenses can quickly spiral into debt, crushing any momentum toward wealth creation. Therefore, financial prudence dictates that an emergency fund with at least three to six months of living expenses be prioritized before more aggressive investing or spending plans are pursued. This fund not only offers peace of mind but also serves as a solid foundation on which all other financial structures can be confidently built.

Beyond emergencies, saving also lays the groundwork for wealth growth. The secret lies in transforming the act of saving from a passive endeavor into an active strategy that leverages compound interest and disciplined accumulation. High-yield savings accounts, certificates of deposit, or money market funds are useful tools in this endeavor—they provide safe havens where money can grow modestly while remaining accessible. However, saving must transcend being a mere reservoir for funds and evolve into a launchpad for investments and wealth multiplication. This shift requires understanding the delicate balance between liquidity and growth potential, choosing the right mix to match one's risk tolerance, timeframe, and financial goals. The discipline of automating savings is crucial here; by arranging automatic transfers to savings accounts or investment vehicles immediately upon receipt of income, one fences off funds from impulsive spending while institutionalizing a habit that will yield exponential benefits over time.

Beyond the mechanics of recording income and expenses, the psychological dimension of budgeting and saving profoundly influences one's success. Many individuals grapple with deeply ingrained beliefs around money, often rooted in childhood experiences or cultural narratives that shape their financial behaviors. For instance, scarcity mentalities can trigger fear-based spending or avoidance of accounting, while affluence mindsets open one up to proactive management and conscious accumulation. Emotional spending—using money to soothe stress or validate self-worth—poses a significant hurdle in saving progress, as it disconnects expenditure from rational decision-making. Addressing these underlying emotional currents requires self-reflection and sometimes confronting uncomfortable feelings, yet such introspection is critical to forging lasting financial habits. Budgeting tools that incorporate behavioral nudges—like setting personalized savings goals or visualizing the impact of financial choices—can help bridge the gap between intention and action, transforming budgeting from a chore into an empowering daily ritual.

Technological advancements have revolutionized the way budgeting and saving are approached, making the process infinitely more accessible and data driven. Financial management apps that sync directly with bank accounts offer real-time visibility into spending patterns, automated categorization, and alerts that flag potential overspending before it occurs. These tools not only save time but also reduce cognitive load, making budget adherence more feasible amid busy lives. Moreover, they provide visual dashboards that track progress toward savings goals, enabling motivation through tangible milestones. Coupling technology with human discipline creates a powerful synergy—where insights fuel smarter choices and accountability structures sustain consistency. Yet, while such digital tools democratize access to sophisticated financial management, they do not replace the need for a clear strategy and steadfast commitment. Technology is an enabler, not a substitute for financial wisdom.

Crafting a robust savings strategy demands mindful decisions about where to allocate funds for maximum impact. Prioritization naturally emerges as an indispensable aspect, particularly when resources are limited. Debt serves as a pivotal crossroads in these decisions. High-interest debts, like credit card balances, are wealth killers that siphon off resources through exorbitant interest charges and fees, often dwarfing potential returns from saving or investing. The mathematical and psychological relief of eliminating such debt should be pursued aggressively before diverting significant funds toward saving or investing. Conversely, low-interest debt, such as certain mortgages or student loans, may constitute a manageable risk if balanced with concurrent savings, especially in environments where inflation or investment returns outpace interest rates. Recognizing these nuances enables a customized approach that optimizes resource deployment instead of subscribing blindly to one-size-fits-all advice.

Once debts are responsibly managed, the next frontier is to explore strategies that inject intentional growth into savings. The power of compound interest cannot be overstated; it transforms modest, consistent contributions into formidable wealth over decades. This outcome illustrates a fundamental principle of wealth creation: starting early and maintaining discipline trump attempts at timing the market or chasing speculative gains. Creating multiple "buckets" of savings—each with distinct purposes, liquidity requirements, and risk profiles—sharpens focus and reduces the instinct to raid funds prematurely. For example, a short-term bucket kept in accessible but low-yield accounts funds planned expenses like holidays or home repairs, while a long-term bucket invested in diversified portfolios of stocks and bonds targets retirement and legacy wealth. This segmentation helps resist temptation and aligns cash flow management with specific life stages and aspirations.

Cultivating discipline in budgeting and saving also hinges on the ability to resist societal pressures that equate spending with status or happiness. Modern consumer culture tempts individuals to live beyond their means, often masking financial instability behind a veneer of appearances. The wealth-building mindset flips this script, viewing frugality not as limitation but as liberation, a conscious choice to prioritize future security and freedom. True wealth, after all, is not the number of possessions or the flashiness of lifestyle, but the serenity that comes from financial autonomy. That serenity allows for making life choices based on purpose rather than necessity. It requires discipline to live below one's means consistently, avoid lifestyle inflation—a tendency to increase spending in tandem with income—and follow an intentional trajectory where consumption habits serve strategic saving and investing.

An often-underestimated aspect of budgeting and saving is the role of relationships and communication. Financial decisions rarely exist in isolation, especially within families or partnerships where joint income, goals, and responsibilities must be harmonized. Establishing open, transparent conversations around money fosters mutual accountability and alignment on priorities. It also diffuses misunderstandings and reduces secretive behaviors that often undermine long-term planning. Joint budgeting sessions or financial check-ins become opportunities not only for planning but for reinforcing shared values and vision. In this way, budgeting acts as both a financial tool and a relational practice, binding families and partners through shared commitment to wealth creation and security.

Understanding financial instruments available for saving amplifies the effectiveness of budgeting. Beyond the basic savings account, tools like individual retirement accounts (IRAs), 401(k) plans, health savings accounts (HSAs), and education savings plans offer tax advantages and growth potential that maximizes the value of every saved dollar. Grasping these options enables individuals to tailor portfolios according to personal circumstances and future needs. For example, taking advantage of employer-sponsored retirement plans, especially those with matching contributions, effectively doubles the impact of saving efforts. The interplay between budgeting and leveraging these instruments is critical—it's one thing to put money away, it's another to deploy it intelligently to harness market growth, mitigate taxes, and hedge against inflation. A well-structured budget anticipates these instruments, allocating funds not just for short-term stability but long-term prosperity.

A few practical strategies exemplify effective budgeting and saving execution. First, "paying yourself first" is a paradigm shift in managing money—prioritizing savings automatically each month before other expenses ensures that financial goals are met consistently rather than waiting for leftovers. Additionally, reviewing and adjusting the budget regularly keeps strategies responsive to life's changes, such as fluctuating income, evolving goals, or unexpected expenses. Flexibility within discipline allows for sustainability. Another transformative approach is embracing minimalism, where simplifying one's lifestyle directly trims spending and increases capacity to save. It's not about sacrifice in hardship but about valuing quality and purpose over quantity or impulse. Finally, cultivating financial literacy is essential: understanding terms, trends, and principles empowers individuals to defend their wealth against misinformation and make informed choices confidently.

The journey of budgeting and saving is fundamentally a journey of empowerment and transformation. It moves individuals from reactive money management, often characterized by stress and scarcity, to proactive stewardship characterized by confidence and growth. This transformation is not instantaneous but a gradual unfolding, fostered by consistent habits, reflection, and education. Each dollar saved is a vote cast for the future you desire—a future where financial freedom fuels dreams and not just survival. As the bedrock of all wealth-building efforts, budgeting and saving forge a resilient platform upon which to build an enduring legacy. Embracing these practices with intentionality ignites a virtuous cycle: the more control you assert today, the more options and freedom you secure for tomorrow, revealing the profound power locked within every financial decision made with clarity and purpose.

Chapter 3: Basics of Investing

"The stock market is a device for transferring money from the impatient to the patient." — Warren Buffett

Key Takeaways

- Investing allows your money to grow over time.
- Risk and return are closely connected.
- Diversification reduces investment risk.
- Long-term investing generally outperforms short-term speculation.
- Understanding your risk tolerance is essential.
- Consistency often matters more than timing the market.
- Investing should align with your financial goals.

Investing is often heralded as the cornerstone of building lasting wealth, yet for many, the very idea of investing conjures images of complex jargon, intimidating charts, and financial markets governed by inscrutable forces. However, at its core, investing is far simpler and fundamentally about making your money work for you. Before diving into specific vehicles, it's essential to understand the basic principles that govern investing — primarily the intertwined relationship between risk and return, the nature of different investment options, and how they fit into a broader financial strategy designed to increase your net worth over time.

Imagine a garden where seeds you plant have the potential to grow into fruitful plants. Some seeds may sprout quickly but yield less produce, while others take longer to mature but offer abundant harvests for years. Investing works similarly. When you place your money in different assets, you are essentially planting seeds that will grow, but the growth varies depending on the type of asset and the risk involved. Risk in investing, refers to the possibility that the actual return on an investment will differ from the expected return — this includes the chance of losing some or all the invested capital. Return, conversely, is the money you gain or lose on an investment over a period. Every investment contains a trade-off between risk and return: generally, the higher the expected return, the greater the risk you assume.

There is no such thing as an investment devoid of risk. Even the safest kinds carry some level of uncertainty. For example, government bonds are widely considered low risk because they are backed by the full faith and credit of the issuing government. While they offer relatively modest returns, the likelihood of their default is minimal compared to stocks of a startup company that could yield high returns but also run the risk of failure.

Recognizing your own tolerance for risk — shaped by your financial goals, time horizon, emotional makeup, and liquidity needs — is the first step toward effectively navigating investment choices. The balance between risk and reward is not static; it must be reassessed as your personal circumstances, and market conditions evolve.

Turning to investment vehicles, it is important to start with the basics. The most common types of investments include stocks, bonds, mutual funds, exchange-traded funds (ETFs), real estate, commodities, and cash equivalents. Stocks are ownership shares in a company. By purchasing stock, you become a partial owner entitled to a share of the company's profits and assets. Stocks typically offer the highest potential returns among common investments but with significant variability and volatility. This makes them suitable for investors with a longer time horizon and a greater appetite for risk. Bonds, on the other hand, are essentially loans you make to organizations, governments, municipalities, or corporations—in exchange for periodic interest payments plus the return of the bond's face value at maturity. Bonds tend to be less volatile than stocks, providing steady income and preservation of capital, albeit with generally lower returns.

Mutual funds and ETFs serve as pooled investment vehicles, allowing individuals to own a diversified portfolio managed by professionals. Mutual funds collect money from many investors to buy a broad range of securities, while ETFs often mimic specific indices and trade on stock exchanges like individual stocks. These funds can either focus on stocks, bonds, or a combination of asset classes, helping reduce the risk associated with investing in single securities by diversifying across many investments. The appeal lies in lower barriers to entry, diversification, and professional management, making them ideal for beginners who want exposure to the market without needing to handpick individual securities.

Real estate investment can take many forms, from purchasing physical properties to owning shares in real estate investment trusts (REITs). Direct real estate ownership offers potential for rental income and capital appreciation but requires substantial capital, management effort, and comes with liquidity challenges. REITs provide a more liquid and accessible way to invest in real estate markets without the hassle of property management, offering income streams generated from commercial or residential property portfolios. Commodities such as gold, silver, oil, and agricultural products offer another category of investments, often used for diversification and hedging against inflation or economic downturns. However, commodity prices can be highly volatile and affected by geopolitical events, supply-demand imbalances, and market speculation.

Cash equivalents, including money market funds and certificates of deposit (CDs), provide the lowest risk and lowest returns in the spectrum. They are highly liquid and stable but offer minimal growth potential, making them useful as a place to park funds for short-term needs or emergency reserves. Understanding where these investments lie on the risk-return continuum and what role they play in achieving your financial objectives is crucial. A well-balanced investment portfolio typically mixes assets with varying degrees of risk and correlation to smooth out the ride through changing economic cycles and market conditions.

While the diversity of investment options might seem overwhelming at first glance, the fundamentals bring clarity: each investment vehicle possesses unique features that determine its suitability based on your goals, risk tolerance, and time horizon. For example, a young professional prioritizing long-term growth could favor stocks and equity funds to harness the power of compound growth over decades. In contrast, a person nearing retirement might shift allocations toward bonds and cash equivalents to preserve accumulated wealth and ensure income stability. This dynamic allocation is sometimes referred to as asset allocation, arguably one of the most important determinants of investment success. It involves distributing your funds across various asset classes to achieve the optimal balance of risk and return customized to your circumstances.

The concept of compounding further reinforces why investing early and consistently is critical. The magic of compounding lies in earning returns not only on your initial investment but also on the reinvested earnings over time. Albert Einstein reportedly called compound interest the "eighth wonder of the world," emphasizing its ability to exponentially increase wealth the longer it is allowed to work. This is why even modest contributions made regularly toward investments can grow into substantial sums—patience and persistence are essential virtues in the investment journey.

Additionally, it is vital to recognize the impact of fees, costs, and taxes on your investment returns. High management fees can erode your gains over time, especially in mutual funds with aggressive fee structures. Similarly, taxes on dividends, interest, and capital gains reduce the net return that lands in your pocket. Understanding tax-advantaged accounts like IRAs, 401(k)s, or other retirement vehicles can mitigate this burden, allowing your investments to grow more efficiently. In some cases, long-term capital gains tax rates are lower than those on ordinary income, providing incentives to hold investments longer and avoid short-term trading.

Investors must also grapple with market psychology – the emotional forces that drive buying and selling decisions often detached from fundamental values. Fear and greed can lead to swings in prices, resulting in market bubbles or crashes. A sound investment approach involves discipline and adherence to a well-crafted plan rather than succumbing to impulsive trades driven by market noise. Dollar-cost averaging, which entails investing fixed amounts regularly regardless of market fluctuations, is a strategy that can reduce the risk of mistiming the market and build wealth steadily.

Beyond tangible mechanics, investing demands a mindset shift from short-term gratification to long-term orientation. Viewing your investments as parts of an evolving narrative where patience, resilience, continuous learning, and strategic adjustments shape your financial destiny is critical. Wealth creation is not merely a technical exercise but one that intertwines with your broader life goals, values, and aspirations.

In conclusion, the basics of investing rest on embracing the balance between risk and reward, understanding the variety of investment vehicles, and appreciating how these elements fit into a cohesive strategy tailored to your personal financial situation. By demystifying terms like stocks, bonds, mutual funds, and highlighting the significance of compounding, diversification, asset allocation, and disciplined investing behavior, you lay a solid foundation for your financial future. The path to wealth begins with informed decisions that respect your capacity for risk and your vision for the future, each investment choice is a step toward turning potential into tangible financial security and freedom. With this knowledge, you are empowered to craft a confident, purposeful journey on the road to lasting prosperity.

Chapter 4: Understanding Debt and Credit

"Beware of little expenses. A small leak will sink a great ship." — Benjamin Franklin

Key Takeaways

- Not all debt is harmful; distinguish between good and bad debt.
- Credit should be managed responsibly.
- High-interest debt delays wealth creation.
- Paying bills on time protects your credit score.
- Borrow only for productive purposes.
- Eliminating unnecessary debt improves financial freedom.
- Strong credit opens doors to future opportunities.

In the intricate journey toward financial freedom, understanding the nuanced relationship between debt and credit is paramount. These two financial instruments, often misunderstood and maligned, wield immense power to shape the trajectory of one's wealth if managed wisely. Debt, when handled irresponsibly, can become a crippling force; yet, when leveraged strategically, it can serve as a vital catalyst for wealth creation. Similarly, credit represents opportunity—to bridge that connects present resources with future gain—but requires discipline and insight to harness effectively. To navigate this landscape proficiently, one must first demystify what debt and credit truly embody, disentangling common misconceptions and replacing fear with knowledge grounded in practical awareness.

Debt is frequently painted in dark hues—a burden, a trap, a looming threat to financial security. However, such a narrow perspective fails to account for the multifaceted nature of debt. At its core, debt is simply borrowed money, a tool by which individuals or entities access funds they do not currently possess. This borrowed capital often comes with a cost, expressed as interest, which compensates the lender for risk and opportunity cost. Yet, debt is distinguished not just by its existence but by its quality and purpose. The critical difference lies between 'good debt' and 'bad debt.' Good debt is an investment in income-generating assets or growth opportunities—such as education loans enhancing earning potential, business loans fueling entrepreneurship, or mortgages on properties that appreciate. Bad debt, conversely, often finances depreciating liabilities like excessive credit card balances spent on discretionary consumption or loans for rapidly losing value assets. Recognizing and adopting this lens allows one to see debt not merely as an obstacle but as a resource to be strategically utilized.

Credit, intertwined intimately with debt, refers to the trust extended to a borrower by a lender wherein the borrower is allowed access to funds or services under the promise to repay later. A credit profile encapsulates one's financial reputation and preparedness, influencing access to varied financial opportunities, from everyday purchases to substantial investments. The credit score, a numerical distillation of one's creditworthiness, profoundly impacts the cost of borrowing. High credit scores translate to favorable loan terms, lower interest rates, and greater financial flexibility, whereas poor scores limit options and increase costs. Understanding the mechanics behind credit scores—the factors contributing to them, such as payment punctuality, credit utilization ratios, length of credit history, diversity of credit types, and recent credit inquiries—is crucial. Armed with this understanding, individuals can take proactive steps to nurture and repair their credit standing, unlocking enduring benefits that ripple across their financial lives.

Managing credit responsibly demands more than passive awareness; it requires deliberate, disciplined behavior and strategic foresight. One essential component involves prudent use of revolving credit facilities like credit cards. While these instruments offer convenience and can augment purchasing power, they also carry the potential for rapid debt accumulation if unchecked. Keeping credit utilization—the proportion of available credit used—below recommended thresholds not only safeguards credit scores but also signals financial prudence to potential lenders. Paying full balances monthly, or at least consistently exceeding minimum payments, prevents the accrual of high-interest charges that erode financial health over time. Additionally, avoiding the temptation to treat credit as 'free money' instills discipline vital for sustainable wealth accumulation.

Leveraging debt responsibly also entails a keen understanding of loan structures, interest calculations, and repayment schedules. Loans come in diverse forms—fixed-rate mortgages, variable-rate personal loans, auto loans, student loans, lines of credit—and each type carries unique features influencing total cost and flexibility. For example, fixed-interest loans provide stability in repayment amounts, shielding borrowers from market fluctuations, while variable rates may offer lower initial costs but expose them to rising interest burdens. Understanding amortization, the breakdown of principal and interest over time, empowers borrowers to strategize prepayments and reduce long-term liabilities. Furthermore, timing and sequencing debt repayment are critical; prioritizing high-interest debts accelerates financial liberation by minimizing interest outflows, freeing up cash flows for investment or saving. Employing methods such as the avalanche approach—tackling debts with the highest interest rates first—or the snowball method—focusing on smaller debts to build momentum—helps tailor repayment strategies to psychological and financial contexts.

Beyond individual tactics, the role of credit and debt must be viewed within the broader framework of overall financial health. Building a resilient personal economy involves integrating credit and debt management with budgeting, emergency fund establishment, and investment planning. A well-crafted budget aligns income with expenses, creating surplus cash flow that reduces reliance on credit and facilitates disciplined debt repayment. An emergency fund acts as a buffer against unforeseen circumstances, preventing impulsive borrowing and the cascade of debt spiraling from crises. Moreover, as one's financial foundation strengthens, the prospect of using leverage—borrowing to amplify investment returns—becomes viable. Here, understanding the risk-reward equation is imperative; leveraging debt amplifies gains but equally magnifies losses, underscoring the necessity of prudent risk management.

Today's financial environment is also shaped by evolving technology and data analytics, which influence credit availability, lending criteria, and debt management tools. Digital platforms provide unprecedented access to credit reports, automated payment reminders, and personalized financial coaching, empowering consumers with insights previously available only to professionals. Harnessing these resources enhances financial literacy and fosters proactive management of credit profiles. Equally, leveraging technological innovations such as artificial intelligence-driven budgeting apps and robo-advisors can optimize debt repayment strategies, simulate outcomes, and identify opportunities to refinance or consolidate high-cost debts at better terms. This intersection of financial discipline and technology creates fertile ground for sustainable growth and informed borrowing.

At its ethical core, managing debt and credit responsibly requires cultivating a mindset oriented toward long-term financial well-being rather than short-term gratification. It involves resisting cultural pressures that glorify consumption and instant access to expensive goods without corresponding means. Embracing a philosophy that prioritizes living within one's means, coupled with a strategic approach to borrowing, redefines financial freedom as the state of controlled resources rather than merely higher income or assets. This shift transforms debt from a source of stress to a strategic tool—when used judiciously, it can accelerate wealth creation and deepen financial independence.

Stories abound of individuals and families trapped under mountains of debt, struggling to recover from reckless borrowing. Conversely, equally compelling are tales of entrepreneurs who leveraged credit lines to seize market opportunities, workers who financed education to break cycles of poverty, and investors who used mortgage debt to build substantial real estate portfolios. These narratives, diverse and instructive, illuminate the pathway from financial vulnerability to empowerment. They underscore a universal truth: understanding and mastering debt and credit mechanics is not just about numbers but about translating knowledge into intentional actions that align with personal values and ambitions.

In practical terms, cultivating this mastery begins with education and deliberate self-assessment. Beginning with a detailed examination of one's credit report, identifying inaccuracies, and understanding historical borrowing behavior lays the groundwork for transformation. Setting clear financial goals provides the compass for credit use—whether that is qualifying for a home loan, starting a business, or building an emergency fund. Monitoring progress against these goals, adjusting behaviors to reduce unnecessary borrowing and improve repayment discipline, and engaging with financial advisors or mentors, when necessary, strengthens accountability. Engaging in continual financial education, staying abreast of changes in credit scoring models, lending market conditions, and regulatory environments ensure adaptability and resilience.

Ultimately, understanding debt and credit within the broader narrative of wealth building reframes these tools as integral components of a holistic financial strategy. They interplay dynamically with mindset, skills, relationships, and technological advances, each influencing and amplifying the others. Mastery of debt and credit is not an end but a catalyst—one that, when intertwined with purposeful growth and ethical stewardship, propels individuals beyond mere survival into realms of prosperity and lasting financial freedom. Embracing this responsibility, with clarity and courage, transforms the abstract concepts of debt and credit into concrete steppingstones on the path toward a future defined by security, opportunity, and fulfillment.

Chapter 5:
Skill Building for Career Success

"Formal education will make you a living; self-education will make you a fortune." — Jim Rohn

Key Takeaways

- Your skills determine your earning potential.
- Continuous improvement increases career opportunities.
- Technical and soft skills are equally important.
- Learning should become a lifelong habit.
- Employers reward competence and adaptability.
- Investing in yourself produces the highest returns.
- Career growth begins with personal growth.

Identifying High-Demand Skills

In the vast landscape of career development and wealth creation, the pursuit of high-demand skills stands as a pivotal cornerstone. These are not merely competencies acquired by chance or whim; rather, they are dynamic capabilities deeply intertwined with the evolving currents of the marketplace, technological innovation, and human needs. Recognizing and cultivating such skills requires more than casual observation; it demands a deliberate, thoughtful approach rooted in awareness, adaptability, and strategic foresight. The question then becomes: how does one navigate this complex terrain to identify those skills that truly enhance market value and, consequently, career trajectory and financial freedom?

To begin uncovering high-demand skills, it is essential to shift the lens from a passive accumulation of knowledge to an active engagement with the pulse of the global economy. This starts with observing emerging industries, technological trends, and shifts in consumer behavior. For example, the rapid rise of artificial intelligence, data science, renewable energy, and digital marketing highlights sectors where expertise is not just desired but indispensable. However, understanding these macro trends only scratches the surface. One must delve deeper into the skills that act as the currency within these domains. It is not enough to know that artificial intelligence is booming; one must discern the skills—such as machine learning algorithms, natural language processing, or ethical AI implementation—that employers, entrepreneurs, and innovators seek. This process transforms a general awareness into actionable intelligence, setting the stage for targeted skill acquisition.

Simultaneously, the modern job market's fluidity necessitates awareness of how skills transfer across industries and roles. Increasingly, hybrid skills are commanding premium value—combinations of technical expertise and soft skills like emotional intelligence, leadership, communication, and adaptability. For instance, an IT professional who also has a master's in project management and client relations becomes a multifaceted asset, capable of bridging gaps between technical teams and business objectives. Developing this layered skill set not only expands opportunities but also fortifies resilience against market disruptions. Thoughtful introspection coupled with external research—engaging with industry reports, job postings, and thought leader analyses—can reveal these intricate patterns, helping individuals tailor their growth trajectory toward versatile, high-impact competencies.

The journey toward identifying market-relevant skills is significantly enriched by continuous learning. In an era where knowledge halts its forward march within months, static skillsets become liabilities rather than assets. Cultivating a mindset geared toward perpetual education creates a powerful advantage. This involves embracing formal avenues like accredited courses, certifications, and advanced degrees, as well as informal mechanisms such as webinars, podcasts, online forums, and peer workshops. Importantly, this educational pursuit should not be random or driven by fad-chasing; instead, it must be strategic and aligned with carefully researched career goals. For example, if data analytics emerge as a prospective domain of interest, the learner should seek masterclasses in data visualization, statistical programming languages, and real-world case studies to build a robust, market-ready foundation. This layered approach ensures depth and relevance, separating superficial familiarity from genuine expertise that employers trust.

Networking emerges as another indispensable dimension in the quest to pinpoint and develop high-demand skills. Connections within professional communities act as living repositories of knowledge, reflecting current demands and offering insights not easily captured through impersonal research alone. Engaging with mentors, attending industry conferences, participating actively in online professional groups, and seeking feedback from colleagues create avenues for real-time intelligence on skill trends. These interactions often illuminate subtle shifts before they become mainstream—whether a new coding framework gaining traction or a leadership approach resonating within startup ecosystems. Moreover, networking cultivates opportunities for collaborations, apprenticeships, and project experiences that translate learning into demonstrable competence. The relational fabric woven through these engagements often becomes a springboard for career advancement, as reputational capital grows alongside skill mastery.

Strategic positioning within the job market is the third pillar that transforms skill recognition into tangible career gains. Possessing relevant skills is no guarantee of opportunity without visibility and alignment with demand. Building a personal brand, both online and offline, plays a crucial role here. Thoughtful curation of professional profiles, portfolios, and social media presences signals not only expertise but also commitment and vision. Sharing content, contributing to discussions, and showcasing projects creates a narrative of value that attracts recruiters, clients, and collaborators alike. Additionally, identifying niche areas where one can become a recognized authority increases leverage. For example, a marketer specializing in sustainable brand promotion or a developer focused on fintech blockchain applications occupies a space less crowded but highly sought after. This conscious narrowing coupled with relentless quality elevates one's market value beyond generic competencies.

Equally important is the cultivation of a growth mindset—a psychological framework pioneered by Carol Dweck that views abilities as malleable through effort and learning. Individuals who embrace this perspective approach skill acquisition as an evolving journey rather than a fixed checklist. They become agile learners, capable of shifting trajectories as market demands fluctuate. This mindset encourages experimentation, risk-taking, and resilience in the face of setbacks, all of which are vital in mastering complex skills and standing out in competitive environments. It also fosters curiosity about adjacent disciplines and technological advancements, building a well-rounded portfolio of capabilities that adapt fluidly to the future of work.

Practical application is another critical factor that transforms abstract skill concepts into market-ready assets. Skills—regardless of their demand—lose value if not demonstrated through real-world projects, internships, or entrepreneurial ventures. Opportunities to apply knowledge consolidate understanding and build confidence, while generating tangible proof of competency. Engaging in freelance work, volunteering for relevant projects, or initiating passion projects can serve this purpose exceptionally well. These experiences often lead to the formation of a professional narrative that resonates deeply with employers, illustrating problem-solving capabilities, adaptability, and initiative. In turn, this practical groundwork attracts higher-level responsibilities and remuneration, accelerating financial growth and career progression.

In parallel, self-assessment and reflective practices enable individuals to continually calibrate their skill-building efforts. Regularly evaluating strengths and gaps, soliciting constructive feedback, and revisiting personal goals ensure alignment with evolving ambitions and market realities. This introspective cycle guards against complacency, fosters intentionality, and highlights emerging opportunities for development. Tools such as skill assessments, 360-degree reviews, and mentorship sessions provide structured avenues for this reflection. By integrating these insights, individuals maintain a trajectory that is both ambitious and grounded, optimizing the return on investment in learning efforts.

Another facet to consider is the role of technology in accelerating skill acquisition and enhancing marketability. Digital platforms democratize access to knowledge and networking, breaking barriers of geography and socioeconomic background. Platforms like LinkedIn, Coursera, Udemy, and Khan Academy offer curated, accessible paths to emerging skills, while virtual conferences and webinars facilitate global connection among professionals. Leveraging technology also enables tracking industry trends via analytics tools, setting up alerts for job opportunities that match skill growth, and engaging in virtual collaboration that mirrors future work environments. Thus, digital literacy itself becomes a meta-skill that amplifies the capacity to discover, learn, and demonstrate high-demand skills effectively.

Furthermore, the interplay between industry certifications and experiential learning enriches the profile of a skilled professional. Certifications signal verified competence and provide credibility in competitive markets, while hands-on experience ensures practical know-how and adaptability. For example, obtaining a Project Management Professional (PMP) certification complements actual management of complex projects, reflecting both theoretical understanding and applied expertise. Strategic planning around when and which certifications to pursue thus becomes a critical decision, aligned with long-term goals rather than impulsive credentialism. This balance nurtures a well-rounded, resilient professional profile that commands higher market value.

The emergence of soft skills as equally indispensable elements of high-demand skill portfolios cannot be overstated. In an era increasingly dominated by automation of routine tasks, human-centric skills—empathy, critical thinking, collaboration, and emotional intelligence—have surged in importance. These qualities enhance teamwork, leadership, customer engagement, and innovation, enriching technical capacity with relational depth. Cultivating such attributes requires intentional practice, self-awareness, and often mentorship, as they evolve through interactions and experiences rather than formal study alone. Professionals who harmonize technical prowess with strong interpersonal skills stand apart in the marketplace, positioning themselves for roles that influence culture, strategy, and growth.

Cross-cultural competency and global awareness also augment the value of high-demand skills in an interconnected economy. As businesses expand across borders and remote teams become standard, the ability to navigate diverse environments, communicate effectively across cultures, and appreciate global dynamics grows critical. This skill set includes linguistic proficiency, cultural intelligence, and adaptability to various business practices and regulatory frameworks. Building such competence involves travel, interaction with international peers, and dedicated study of global trends—activities that not only enhance employability but also enrich personal growth and worldview.

Finally, the ethical dimensions of skill application warrant attention in identifying truly valuable competencies. Skills wielded without integrity or purpose may generate short-term gains but fail to build lasting wealth or impact. Integrating ethical considerations into skill development and deployment ensures alignment with broader personal and societal values, fostering trust, reputation, and sustainable relationships. For instance, a data scientist committed to privacy rights and fairness in algorithm design exemplifies this principle, contributing both to career success and social good. This fusion of competence and character represents a higher order of market value, differentiating professionals as principled leaders in their fields.

In summary, identifying high-demand skills entails a comprehensive blend of market awareness, continuous learning, networking, strategic positioning, growth mindset, practical application, reflection, technological leverage, certification, soft skills cultivation, global competency, and ethical grounding. This multifaceted approach not only reveals what skills are relevant but also how to cultivate them in ways that create meaningful career advancement and robust financial freedom. The journey is ongoing, adaptive, and requires intentionality, but it returns profound dividends by transforming individuals into indispensable contributors within the evolving world of work. As you embark on this path, remember that the power to build and sustain wealth begins with mastering the art of learning and leveraging the skills that demand will recognize and reward.

Chapter 6:
Continuous Learning and Adaptability

"The illiterate of the twenty-first century will not be those who cannot read and write, but those who cannot learn, unlearn, and relearn." — Alvin Toffler

Key Takeaways

- Learning never stops in a changing economy.
- Adaptability is a competitive advantage.
- Curiosity drives innovation.
- Technology requires continuous upskilling.
- Embrace change rather than resist it.
- Every challenge presents a learning opportunity.
- Lifelong learners remain valuable in every industry.

In an ever-evolving world, where the only constant is change itself, the ability to learn continuously and adapt swiftly becomes not just an asset but a necessity for anyone determined to build lasting wealth and secure their financial future. The landscape of work, entrepreneurship, and leadership is in perpetual flux, reshaped by technological innovation, shifting societal demands, and the unpredictable rhythms of global markets. To navigate this complexity successfully, you must cultivate a mindset and lifestyle deeply anchored in lifelong learning, self-reflection, and strategic adaptability. Continuous learning is far more than simply acquiring knowledge; it is about transforming how you engage with the world, how you perceive challenge and opportunity, and how you shape your own relevance in an environment that seems to accelerate in its pace and unpredictability every day.

At its core, continuous learning demands humility—the recognition that no matter how much you've achieved or how skilled you currently are, there is always room for growth and renewal. This realization shifts learning from being a sporadic or reactive act into an intrinsic, proactive part of your identity. As the world reinvents the very nature of work through artificial intelligence, automation, and digital platforms, remaining stagnant is tantamount to obsolescence. Traditional professions decline while new roles emerge, often demanding sets of skills that did not exist five years prior. An economist's prediction today is a stark warning: the jobs of tomorrow belong to those who can adapt, unlearning outdated methodologies while embracing new competencies with enthusiasm and agility.

To weave continuous learning into the fabric of your everyday life, it is useful to envision learning as a vast ecosystem rather than a series of isolated educational events. Start with the understanding that learning occurs through multiple channels: formal education, hands-on experience, mentorship, self-directed study, digital consumption, critical reflection, and collaborative exchange. Each of these channels, when cultivated deliberately, becomes a powerful vehicle for staying ahead of the curve. For example, online platforms offering courses, tutorials, and seminars have democratized access to education, breaking geographical and economic barriers and making high-quality learning materials accessible instantly. But passive consumption of content is insufficient. True learning emerges from engagement—applying new concepts, testing ideas in real-world scenarios, seeking feedback, and iterating.

Furthermore, the quest for continuous learning comes together with adaptability in mindset and behavior. To be adaptable means embracing discomfort as a necessary catalyst for growth. It calls for the development of psychological flexibility—an openness to change coupled with resilience when confronted by setbacks or unfamiliar situations. Those who cling rigidly to old paradigms or resist the discomfort of entering unknown territory risk being sidelined by more flexible and resourceful peers. Adaptability shows itself not only in the willingness to learn new skills but also in the readiness to pivot strategic directions, adopt novel technologies, and rethink personal goals in response to new information or shifting circumstances.

Networking plays a pivotal role in this continuous adaptation cycle because no one learns or adapts entirely in isolation. In today's knowledge-driven economy, relationships are conduits of insight, opportunity, and collaboration. Curating a diverse and dynamic network exposes you to perspectives and innovations that challenge your assumptions and spark novel ideas. It is within these interpersonal exchanges that you can validate what you learn, benchmark your progress, and uncover emerging trends before they become mainstream. Active networking, whether through social media, professional organizations, conferences, or informal gatherings, should be viewed as an ongoing educational journey, a continual renewal of your intellectual and social capital. It is through these interactions that you position yourself strategically in the job market, uncovering opportunities that mere qualifications could never provide.

Positioning oneself strategically entails more than updating a resume or jumping on the latest career bandwagon. It demands a deep self-awareness of strengths, passions, and core values, coupled with a vigilant eye to the currents shaping industries and society at large. Strategic positioning is an iterative process, requiring regular pulse-checks on market demands and personal relevance. Here, the analogy of a chess player proves instructive—anticipating moves not just based on immediate gain but with an eye on long-term positioning.

Which skills will tomorrow's employers prize? Which technologies will render entire sectors obsolete? How do your unique talents intersect with these forces? Reflective questions such as these become vital in crafting a career path that is both resilient and fulfilling.

Beyond technical competencies, cultivating soft skills such as emotional intelligence, effective communication, critical thinking, and creative problem-solving is indispensable in an era defined by collaboration and complexity. These skills often distinguish those who thrive within organizations or marketplaces from those who merely survive. The intangible qualities that deepen human connection and leadership capacity cannot be fully automated or outsourced, which imbues them with increasing value. Thus, an integrated learning approach that develops both hard and soft skills ensures deeper adaptability and broader opportunity.

Importantly, the journey of lifelong learning and adaptability is not linear or uniform for every individual. Learning plateaus, detours, and moments of doubt are inevitable. A sustainable approach involves cultivating curiosity and a growth mindset, celebrating incremental progress, and adopting self-compassion during challenging phases. Reflection becomes a powerful tool; regularly reviewing lessons learned, adapting plans, and setting new learning goals empowers you to maintain momentum. Building learning habits and rituals—such as reading daily, seeking out mentors, dedicating time to skill practice, or journaling insights—makes learning a habitual rhythm rather than an occasional burst.

The digital revolution, with its barrage of information yet unprecedented access, imposes its own demands on effective learning and adaptability. Filtering noise from signals, discerning credible sources, and creating a personalized learning portfolio require critical digital literacy. You must become a savvy curator of information, balancing breadth and depth, and synthesizing diverse viewpoints to build wisdom rather than mere knowledge accumulation. The art of learning in this context is intrinsically linked to discernment and focus—selecting growth areas that align authentically with your goals, values, and real-world applicability, rather than being overwhelmed by endless offerings.

Moreover, as artificial intelligence and machine learning redefine the nature of knowledge work, human learners are invited to evolve in tandem with these systems—not only by acquiring technological fluency but by steering AI applications responsibly and creatively. Engaging with AI tools to amplify your decision-making and productivity represents an advanced form of adaptability, where learning transitions from individual acquisition to symbiotic co-creation with technology. This relationship propels your capacity to innovate and compete, further underscoring the imperative for continuous skill enhancement and open-mindedness.

Ultimately, the commitment to continuous learning and adaptability is more than a strategic career move—it is an expression of personal agency and freedom. By embracing this commitment, you assert control over your financial destiny, transforming potential disruptions into opportunities for reinvention and growth. You no longer remain at the mercy of external turbulence but instead become an active architect of your evolving journey. This empowerment fosters confidence, resilience, and joy, dimensions of wealth that transcend monetary accumulation.

To embody lifelong learning and adaptability, begin with setting clear, actionable goals aligned with your aspirations. Engage in deliberate practice, seek mentorship, immerse yourself in diverse environments, and remain vigilant to the winds of change that sweep through industries and cultures. Accept that the path will reveal new horizons, requiring you to evolve relentlessly. Yet, within this dynamic existence lies the promise of a richer, fuller life where your financial freedom is secured not by chance but by the deliberate, sustained cultivation of your most asset: yourself.

This journey is a continuous cycle of discovery, application, reflection, and reinvention. By mastering these rhythms, you become not only relevant but indispensable, capable of navigating complexity and thriving amid uncertainty. In doing so, you build a foundation of wealth that endures through the shifting tides of the economy and time itself—wealth born from wisdom, discipline, and an unwavering commitment to growth. It is this profound alignment of learning and adaptability that transforms dreams into reality and aspirations into legacy.

Chapter 7:
Networking and Personal Branding

"Your network is your net worth." — *Porter Gale*

Key Takeaways

- Relationships create opportunities.
- Your reputation is one of your greatest assets.
- Networking is about adding value before seeking value.
- Authenticity builds lasting trust.
- Personal branding communicates your unique strengths.
- Strong professional relationships accelerate success.
- Your network can become your net worth.

In the dynamic architecture of career advancement, the twin pillars of networking and personal branding stand as towering constructs upon which lasting professional success is built. Understanding their profound impact begins with recognizing that no individual ascends the ladder of opportunity in isolation. Every opportunity, every breakthrough, and every pivotal moment in one's career is often a reflection of unseen connections and the reputation cultivated over time. Networking is far more than a mere exchange of business cards at a conference or an obligatory handshake at events; it is the art and science of forging meaningful, authentic relationships that can amplify one's influence and open doors to opportunities that remain invisible to the outsider. Personal branding, meanwhile, is the narrative we construct about ourselves in the minds of others—a crafted identity that shapes perceptions and communicates value consistently and compellingly. Together, these forces operate as a synergistic engine propelling careers forward, but their effective deployment requires intentionality, finesse, and a deep commitment to authenticity.

At the heart of networking lies the understanding that it is not the breadth of connections that counts most—but their depth. Quantity without quality is a hollow venture; superficial acquaintances rarely generate the kind of trust and influence necessary to catalyze career breakthroughs. The true power of networking emerges when relationships transcend transactional exchanges and develop into mutually beneficial partnerships grounded in respect, shared goals, and genuine human connection. This requires a shift from viewing networking as a sterile professional chore to embracing it as an ongoing process of engagement, support, and contribution. The most successful networkers are those who listen more than they speak, who seek to understand the aspirations and challenges of others, and who approach relationships with a mindset of generosity rather than self-interest. They invest time and energy in nurturing connections over time, recognizing that trust and reciprocity are built slowly but pay dividends exponentially.

Building a strong network begins with deliberate identification of the communities and individuals aligned with one's career goals. This process involves strategic reflection on where value exchanges are most likely to occur—be it industry associations, professional forums, online platforms, or informal social gatherings. The modern landscape offers a plethora of avenues to establish such connections, from traditional in-person meetings to the nuanced digital corridors of LinkedIn, Twitter, and even niche industry-specific groups. However, regardless of medium, the principles of effective networking remain constant: approach interactions with curiosity, seek common ground, and always be ready to contribute meaningful insights or assistance. Rather than waiting for opportunities to present themselves, proactive networkers create them by fostering dialogues, inviting collaboration, and positioning themselves as valuable nodes within their professional ecosystem.

Personal branding intertwines seamlessly with networking, providing the essential context within which relationships form and evolve. It is the personal brand that lays the groundwork for how one is recognized and remembered. In a crowded marketplace of talent and ambition, a strong personal brand serves as a beacon signaling clarity of purpose, competence, and character. Creating this brand demands introspective clarity about one's unique strengths, values, and aspirations. It is not about fabricating an idealized persona but about amplifying authentic qualities that distinguish an individual from peers. This requires careful articulation of what one stands for, what promise one makes to collaborators or employers, and how consistently that promise is delivered through actions and communications.

Central to personal branding is the narrative, a compelling story that threads together past experiences, current expertise, and future ambitions into a coherent, resonant message. People are naturally drawn to stories; they humanize professionalism and create emotional connections that pure credentials cannot. A well-crafted personal story weaves together challenges overcome, lessons learned, and the unique perspective one brings to the table. This narrative, when shared thoughtfully across networks and platforms, becomes a powerful magnet attracting like-minded collaborators, mentors, and clients. Moreover, it sets the stage for reputation-building by aligning perceptions with the reality of one's skills and character.

In practical terms, personal branding extends beyond content creation into consistent behaviors and engagements. The way one communicates in emails, the tone used in meetings, the reliability in delivering commitments, and the generosity in sharing knowledge—all these contribute silently but powerfully to the brand's substance. Equally important is the visual and digital footprint, from the professional polish of social media profiles to the quality of content shared and the network of followers cultivated. Employers and peers increasingly vet candidates' digital presence before forming opinions, making online consistency a non-negotiable component. Authenticity, however, remains paramount; personal branding that feels contrived or inauthentic is easily discerned and ultimately detrimental. The goal is to project a genuine reflection of one's professional identity, seamlessly integrating personal values with career ambitions.

It is also essential to understand the symbiotic relationship between networking and personal branding in the context of career advancement. Networking opens doors and introduces possibilities, but personal branding ensures that once those doors are opened, the individual is positioned to step confidently through them. One without the other is incomplete; a robust personal brand without an engaged network often means potential goes unseen, while a vast network without a clear brand can lead to missed opportunities or misaligned connections. By nurturing both with equal dedication, individuals create a dynamic ecosystem where relationships and reputation fuel each other, resulting in increased visibility, credibility, and influence.

The process of strategic positioning within the job market through networking and personal branding is also about adaptability and continuous refinement. Careers are no longer linear paths, but dynamic trajectories influenced by shifting market demands, technological advancements, and evolving personal goals. This means that ongoing engagement with one's network and continual evolution of the personal brand are critical. It requires regular assessment of market trends, feedback from trusted peers, and a willingness to innovate one's value proposition. The best networkers and personal brand architects are perpetual learners and experimenters who embrace change as a constant and opportunity.

Moreover, cultivating relationships and personal reputation contributes to an intangible but immensely valuable currency: social capital. Social capital represents the goodwill, trust, and influence accumulated through interpersonal connections. It is a reservoir from which professionals draw when seeking advice, endorsements, collaborations, or new ventures. Unlike financial capital, social capital multiplies as it is invested, rewarding generosity and authenticity. It also serves as a protective buffer during challenging career phases, providing access to support networks and resources. Thus, investing in social capital by nurturing relationships and maintaining a consistent, value-driven personal brand pays long-term dividends far exceeding immediate tangible gains.

In exploring real-world illustrations, the careers of many influential leaders and entrepreneurs underscore the indispensable role of networking and personal branding in their success. Consider an entrepreneur who attends industry conferences not just to promote products but to listen actively, share insights freely, and form collaborative alliances. Over time, these interactions cultivate a reputation for thought leadership and trustworthiness far beyond the transactional. Similarly, professionals who deliberately craft their personal narrative through articles, keynote speeches, and mentoring cultivate a magnetic presence that attracts opportunities aligned with their expertise. These are not happenstance outcomes but the result of deliberate, sustained effort to build both relationships and reputation.

Reflective exercises often reveal that many individuals approach networking with hesitation or superficiality, limiting their potential. Overcoming this barrier involves re-conceptualizing networking not as self-promotion but as an extension of genuine human interaction. By focusing on adding value to others, whether through sharing knowledge, making introductions, or providing encouragement—relationships become natural and fulfilling rather than strained or mechanical. This authentic engagement lays the groundwork for a personal brand that is not self-centered but purpose-driven, enhancing both professional standing and personal satisfaction.

Finally, embracing the interconnected chemistry of networking and personal branding demands an integrated strategy that includes clear goals, intentional actions, and ongoing reflection. It calls for defining what success looks like in concrete terms, identifying key stakeholders and influencers, and developing a communication style that resonates across diverse audiences. Leveraging modern tools such as social media analytics, personal websites, and professional communities can amplify reach, but they must be wielded thoughtfully and humanely. Ultimately, the journey of building relationships and reputation is a continuous one, requiring resilience, humility, and a steadfast commitment to growth. It is through this journey that professionals not only advance their careers but also create meaningful impact, legacy, and purpose—a wealth far richer than the sum of positions or paychecks.

Chapter 8:
Leadership and Influence

"Leadership is not about being in charge. It is about taking care of those in your charge." — *Simon Sinek*

Key Takeaways

- Leadership is built on service, integrity, and vision.
- Influence grows through trust and credibility.
- Great leaders empower others.
- Effective communication strengthens leadership.
- Ethical leadership creates sustainable success.
- Leadership is developed through practice.
- Every person has the potential to lead.

Developing Emotional Intelligence

Within the vast landscape of wealth creation, one element consistently proves itself indispensable yet often underestimated: emotional intelligence. Understanding and managing emotions, both personal and those of others, serve as the bedrock for effective leadership quality that transcends mere transactional financial activities and touches upon the very art of influencing, inspiring, and fostering growth. Emotional intelligence is more than just sensitivity; it encompasses self-awareness, empathy, social skills, and the ability to regulate one's moods and respond to others in ways that build trust and collaboration. These qualities not only shape the character of a leader but also open the gates to new financial prospects and partnerships, transforming the way success is pursued and attained.

At its core, emotional intelligence begins with self-awareness. This is the capacity to recognize and comprehend one's own emotions in real-time, understanding how feelings shape thought patterns and behavior. Many aspiring leaders falter because they lack this foundational insight; they respond impulsively or unconsciously to stressful situations, undermining their credibility and sabotaging opportunities. When a leader is finely attuned to their emotional state, they can engage with challenges from a place of calm reflection rather than reaction. For instance, consider the leader who faces a volatile negotiation. While the immediate impulse might be frustration or defensiveness, an emotionally intelligent individual pauses to identify these feelings, reframing the situation and guiding their response with thoughtful strategy rather than emotion-driven decisions. This nuanced self-regulation fosters resilience—the unshakable strength to persevere amidst uncertainty and pressures common in the business and financial world.

Equally important is empathy—the genuine ability to understand and share the feelings of others. Far from simply being an emotional indulgence, empathy plays a strategic role in leadership dynamics. When a leader demonstrates empathy, they validate the experiences and needs of those they lead, cultivating loyalty and engagement. This is particularly vital in financial endeavors, where trust is currency. Relationships built on empathy tend to be richer and longer lasting, providing access not only to immediate financial returns but also the invaluable networks that propel sustained growth. Imagine an entrepreneur seeking to secure investment; beyond their business acumen and financial projections, it is the capacity to connect authentically with potential partners that often seals the deal. By attuning to the concerns, aspirations, and motivations of investors, the entrepreneur positions their vision as a shared journey rather than a simple transaction. Thus, empathy becomes a bridge, transforming transactional encounters into mutually beneficial partnerships.

The intricate dance of emotions extends further into social skills, the third pillar of emotional intelligence, which involves the ability to navigate social landscapes with finesse. A leader fluent in social interaction can effortlessly inspire and influence others, skillfully managing conflicts and orchestrating collaboration. These social competencies are invaluable when leading teams, negotiating deals, or expanding networks. It is through social skills that abstract strategies manifest into collective action. For example, when a business leader cultivates a culture of open communication and mutual respect, they unlock collective creativity and commitment. In turn, this creates a fertile environment for innovation and financial growth, where ideas and resources flow rather than stagnate. Mastery of social dynamics also empowers leaders to detect subtle cues—reading body language, tone, and unspoken tensions—to preempt conflicts or capitalize on opportunities, demonstrating how emotional intelligence operates as an unseen engine driving effective leadership.

Integral to the exercise of emotional intelligence is decision-making—the very crucible where leadership is tested. Emotions inevitably color our choices, sometimes clouding judgment with biases or prematurely shutting down possibilities. Yet, when harnessed skillfully, emotional awareness enhances decision-making by balancing logic with intuition. Leaders' rich in emotional intelligence understand that decisions shaped solely by cold facts can ignore the human elements embedded in every financial transaction or venture. They recognize that people's fears, hopes, and motivations must inform strategy to ensure alignment and commitment. For example, a decision to pivot a company's direction might be data-driven, but without sensitivity towards employee morale or stakeholder confidence, the transition could implode. By integrating emotional intelligence, leaders create decisions that are both rational and compassionate, increasing the likelihood of successful implementation and sustainable results. This sophisticated approach also includes embracing uncertainty and common terrains in financial innovation—by moderating anxiety and fostering a mindset open to experimentation and adaptation.

Beyond individual capabilities, emotional intelligence profoundly affects a leader's ability to influence others—a skill fundamental to unlocking new financial prospects and partnerships. Influence is not manipulation; it is the art of inspiring confidence and aligning interests in a manner that encourages voluntary collaboration. Leaders who export emotional intelligence model behaviors that engender respect and goodwill, attracting allies and opening doors that wealth alone cannot access. This virtue is especially potent in today's interconnected and fast-evolving economic environment, where alliances can define the trajectory of ventures. Influencing through emotional intelligence involves storytelling that resonates on a human level, articulating visions that inspire, and demonstrating authenticity that dispels skepticism. It transforms networking into genuine relationship-building, creating ecosystems where value flows freely and opportunities abound. For instance, influential leaders often possess the uncanny ability to galvanize cross-sector partnerships, blending resources and expertise that multiply potential returns and mitigate risks.

The advantages of emotional intelligence also extend into conflict management, an unavoidable dimension of leadership and financial dealings. Disputes arise from misaligned expectations, competition, or simple misunderstandings; leaders armed with high emotional intelligence navigate these turbulent waters with skill and grace. By acknowledging emotions—both their own and those of others—such leaders defuse tensions before they escalate and craft resolutions that preserve relationships. This preservation is paramount, as damaged relationships often close off future collaboration and financial growth. Effective conflict resolution through emotional intelligence involves active listening, reflecting feelings, and searching for win-win outcomes, rather than enforcing dominance or capitulation. This approach builds reputational capital, signaling to stakeholders that the leader prioritizes fairness and long-term engagement over short-term gain. In many cases, these resolutions lead to innovative solutions born from diverse perspectives, further embedding emotional intelligence as a driver of creative wealth-building.

Furthermore, emotional intelligence shapes the leader's ability to build and sustain team dynamics—an essential ingredient in scaling financial success. High-performing teams thrive on psychological safety, where members feel valued, heard, and motivated. Leaders who cultivate this environment through empathy, transparent communication, and emotional support unlock the full potential of their people. The financial benefits are profound: teams that feel connected and empowered produce better results, innovate continuously, and exhibit remarkable resilience. Emotional intelligence enables leaders to sense burnout, anxiety, or disengagement within the team, allowing for timely interventions that preserve morale and productivity. Investing in this emotional fabric multiplies returns beyond immediate financial metrics because it generates a culture of trust and collective purpose—key to navigating the inevitable disruptions and challenges in wealth creation.

This emotional dimension becomes particularly salient when leaders confront personal setbacks or failures that test character and resolve. Emotional intelligence equips them to process disappointment constructively, transforming adversity into growth. Such leaders acknowledge their vulnerabilities without being overwhelmed, seek feedback, and realign their purpose with renewed clarity. This recovery not only safeguards their financial trajectory but also models resilience for their followers, further solidifying trust and loyalty. In an era where rapid changes demand agility, this capacity to manage emotional upheaval distinguishes transient success from lasting wealth.

The pathway to developing emotional intelligence is neither simple nor swift; it requires intentional practice and reflection. Self-reflective exercises—journaling emotions, seeking feedback, and mindfulness—help cultivate awareness. Empathy grows through active listening and genuine curiosity about others' perspectives. Social skills develop with conscious engagement in diverse interactions, practicing communication and conflict resolution. Leaders who commit to this developmental process recognize that emotional intelligence is not a static trait but a dynamic competence that flourishes over time, yielding compounded benefits in leadership effectiveness and financial opportunity.

Ultimately, the mastery of emotional intelligence transcends the realm of personal success, extending to the creation of a meaningful legacy. Leaders who weave emotional intelligence into their approach not only accumulate wealth but also nurture ethical frameworks that uplift communities and inspire future generations. Their influence shapes cultures of inclusion, creativity, and purposeful growth—dimensions that enrich financial achievement with profound human significance. This holistic integration, where emotional intelligence acts as the connective thread between mindset, relationships, and strategy, embodies the essence of the wealth equation proposed in this book. It affirms that true financial freedom is inseparable from the wisdom and character that thoughtful, emotionally intelligent leadership fosters.

Chapter 9: Decision-Making Skills

"In any moment of decision, the best thing you can do is the right thing." — Theodore Roosevelt

Key Takeaways

- Good decisions create long-term wealth.
- Analyze facts before acting.
- Emotions should not control financial choices.
- Every decision carries consequences.
- Learn from mistakes without repeating them.
- Strategic thinking improves outcomes.
- Wise decisions compound over time.

Decision-making is the fulcrum upon which effective leadership balances the complexities of business and finance, carving pathways toward growth, sustainability, and meaningful impact. It is an art and a science dance between intuition and analysis, experience and curiosity, courage and caution. At its core, sound decision-making demands more than a quick calculation of risks and rewards; it calls for a deep understanding of oneself, others, and the intricate web of variables that influence outcomes. A leader must be equipped not only with intellectual acumen but also with emotional intelligence, the capacity to comprehend and manage emotions in themselves and in the diverse individuals they interact with. Emotional intelligence is the silent engine that propels clear, confident, and timely decisions, serving as a compass in the turbulent seas of uncertainty and complexity endemic to business and financial environments.

The initial stage of robust decision-making involves careful assessment—not only of external facts such as market trends, financial data, and competitive moves but of internal landscapes as well: personal biases, fears, desires, and blind spots that can cloud judgment. Leaders who understand that their cognition is subject to systematic biases are better prepared to counteract them through deliberate reflection, consultation, and structured processes. For example, the pitfall of confirmation biases the tendency to favor information that confirms preexisting beliefs—can be mitigated by actively seeking dissenting opinions and fostering a culture that values constructive challenge over conformity. This cognitive humility opens the door to more accurate assessments and innovative solutions that would otherwise remain obscured by tunnel vision.

But decision-making transcends mere data crunching; it hinges on the readiness to act swiftly and decisively when necessary. Opportunity often emerges and vanishes within narrow windows, leaving procrastination as an enemy of progress. Leaders who master timeliness understand that paralysis by analysis leads to missed chances while reckless haste invites avoidable mistakes. The equilibrium lies in cultivating a disciplined approach that embraces contingency planning and risk management without becoming mired in over-deliberation. This balance is nurtured through experience, simulation of scenarios, and clear delegation frameworks, all of which empower leaders to move forward with conviction without sacrificing prudence.

Integral to this equation is the nuanced skill of influencing others, a cornerstone of effective decision-making in business and finance. No significant endeavor unfolds in isolation; it is through relationships, partnerships, and networks that ideas evolve into initiatives and ventures flourish into legacies. The ability to persuasively communicate vision, rationale, and benefits gathers allies and mobilizes resources essential to implementation. Influence is not mere manipulation, but an authentic engagement built on trust, empathy, and mutual respect. Leaders who cultivate emotional intelligence excel at tuning into the needs and motivations of stakeholders, adapting their messaging to resonate with diverse audiences without compromising integrity. This empathetic influence creates a fertile environment for collaboration and innovation, drawing people toward collective goals that generate shared financial success.

Moreover, emotional intelligence sharpens one's capacity to manage the interpersonal dynamics inherent in decision-making settings. Negotiations, problem-solving meetings, and strategic discussions often trigger strong emotions—anxiety over risks, excitement about prospects, frustration from setbacks. A leader's ability to remain composed and self-aware while acknowledging and addressing others' feelings diffuses tension and keeps the conversation focused on constructive outcomes. By fostering psychological safety, leaders encourage honest dialogue and creative problem-solving, unleashing the collective intelligence that propels better decisions. Such emotional savvy is crucial in complex financial negotiations, mergers, investments, and partnerships, where stakes are high and interpersonal nuances can tip the scales between success and failure.

Decision-making in business and finance also benefits immensely from the deliberate integration of diverse perspectives. When leaders intentionally seek input from individuals with varying backgrounds, expertise, and worldviews, they build a richer mosaic of information and insight to inform their choices. Diversity serves as a hedge against groupthink and ingrained assumptions, promoting more rigorous scrutiny of options and uncovering hidden risks or opportunities. Encouraging open debate and challenging conventions is not merely a democratic ideal but a pragmatic strategy that enhances decision quality. Leaders who cultivate inclusive environments where dissenting voices are welcomed demonstrate both courage and wisdom—recognizing that the pursuit of excellence often requires navigating discomfort and complexity.

Another crucial decision-making technique is scenario planning, a strategic exercise that envisions multiple possible futures to prepare for uncertainties. By mapping a range of outcomes—optimistic, pessimist, and most likely—leaders create flexible strategies that can adapt to shifting circumstances. This technique counterbalances the natural human tendency toward linear thinking and overconfidence in one preferred scenario. Scenario planning also facilitates proactive resource allocation, risk mitigation, and contingency development, ensuring that decisions are resilient and robust. For instance, a leader considering a substantial investment in a volatile market can craft alternate courses of action depending on fluctuations in regulatory policies, economic cycles, or technological disruption. This foresight empowers decision-makers to navigate complexity with agility rather than react passively to crises.

Equally important is the need to develop a decision-making culture that balances autonomy with accountability. Leaders who micromanage decision processes risk stifling creativity and burdening themselves with an unsustainable load of responsibility. Conversely, distributing decision-making authority empowers individuals closest to the issues to act swiftly and innovatively, fostering ownership and engagement. However, such delegation must be complemented by clear expectations regarding outcomes, transparent communication, and mechanisms for feedback and course correction. This system of responsible autonomy ensures that decisions align with organizational values and strategic objectives while unleashing the collective potential for responsiveness and excellence.

Leadership traits such as resilience, adaptability, and integrity underpin successful decision-making under pressure. The turbulent nature of markets, economies, and technological landscapes guarantees that no decision exists in perfect certainty or permanence. Leaders who embrace uncertainty with resilience view setbacks as learning opportunities rather than failures, maintaining composure and focus amid volatility. Adaptability enables rapid recalibration of strategies in response to new information, shifting conditions, or emerging risks. Integrity ensures that decisions, while ambitious and competitive, adhere to ethical principles and contribute positively to broader societal well-being. This moral backbone not only safeguards reputation but also attracts loyal partners, investors, and customers who value trustworthiness and purpose. Thus, leadership character is inseparable from the fabric of effective decision-making.

The power of reflective practice enhances decision-making skills by promoting continuous learning and self-improvement. After executing decisions, leaders who pause to evaluate outcomes, processes, and their personal judgment develop a feedback loop that refines future choices. This introspection uncovers patterns, strengths, and areas for development, fostering a mindset attuned to growth rather than static competence. Journaling decisions, soliciting candid feedback, and studying both successes and failures enrich this reflective discipline. Over time, such deliberate practice transforms decision-making from a stressful obligation into a confident, dynamic capability that propels leadership effectiveness and business success.

Technology plays an increasingly pivotal role in augmenting decision-making capabilities. Modern leaders harness tools such as artificial intelligence, data analytics, and decision support systems to process vast amounts of information, identify trends, and simulate outcomes with unprecedented speed and precision. These technologies complement human judgment by illuminating insights that might otherwise remain hidden within complex datasets or fast-changing environments. For example, predictive analytics can forecast customer behavior, market shifts, or financial risks, enabling proactive and evidence-based decisions. Yet wise leaders understand that technology is a means, not an end; it amplifies human intuition and discernment without replacing the ethical and relational dimensions integral to sound judgment.

In the realm of finance, decision-making intricately involves balancing short-term exigencies with long-term goals. Financial data may tempt leaders into expedient choices aimed at immediate gains, but seasoned strategists assess implications for capital preservation, growth trajectories, and legacy creation. This temporal awareness guards against strategies that sacrifice sustainability for fleeting victories. Leaders cultivate patience and vision, reframing decisions within broader contexts of resilience and alignment with personal and organizational values. In doing so, they build wealth that is not only quantitative but qualitative, embedded with purpose and durability.

The influence of decision-making extends beyond immediate transactions into the cultivation of reputational capital and strategic partnerships. Leaders who consistently demonstrate sound judgment earn respect and trust in their networks, attracting collaborators, investors, and opportunities that multiply financial prospects. The credibility earned through transparency, accountability, and empathy becomes a powerful currency in negotiations, alliances, and market positioning. Through thoughtful decisions, leaders shape brand identity and stakeholder confidence, creating a virtuous cycle where success breeds further advantage and access.

Finally, decision-making skills flourish most richly within an ecosystem of support and mentorship. No leader operates in isolation; the presence of trusted advisors, peer networks, and coaches provides sound boards, alternative viewpoints, and encouragement. Engaging with such communities sharpens perspective, expands knowledge, and fortifies resolve. Learning from the diverse experiences of others accelerates growth and guards against insularity. Mentorship embodies the transfer of hard-earned wisdom and the modeling of decision-making behaviors that balance ambition with prudence, innovation with ethics.

In sum, cultivating decision-making skills is a multidimensional journey that unites intellectual rigor, emotional intelligence, strategic foresight, and ethical leadership. It demands openness to learning, humility to embrace complexity, and courage to act decisively in the face of uncertainty. The ability to influence others with empathy and integrity, to leverage diverse perspectives and technologies, and to reflect critically on one's judgments builds a robust foundation for enduring financial success. This holistic approach transforms decisions from isolated acts into interconnected steps within a broader wealth equation—one that honors not only material gain but personal values, relationships, and legacy. For the aspiring individual navigating the intricate dance of business and finance, mastering decision-making is less about finding a single "right" answer and more about developing the skillful artistry of choosing wisely, acting boldly, and continuously evolving within a dynamic world.

Chapter 10: Building Influence and Trust

"Trust is the glue of life. It's the foundational principle that holds all relationships." — Stephen R. Covey

Key Takeaways

- Trust is earned through consistency.
- Integrity builds lasting influence.
- Honest relationships strengthen financial opportunities.
- Credibility creates leadership effectiveness.
- Character is more valuable than reputation.
- Trust increases collaboration.
- Ethical behavior always pays long-term dividends.

In the intricate dance of leadership, building influence and trust stands as a foundational pillar, a currency far more valuable than gold or stocks when it comes to shaping opportunities and forging lasting relationships. True leadership transcends positional authority or titles; it is the subtle power of credibility, empathy, and authentic communication that sways hearts and minds. Establishing this kind of influence requires more than just a mastery of technical skills or financial acumen — it demands a deep understanding of human nature and an unwavering commitment to integrity. At its core, influence comes from being perceived as trustworthy, knowledgeable, and worthy of attention. When someone sees you as reliable and principled, they willingly open doors, share resources, and embark on collaborative ventures that multiply wealth and impact exponentially.

Emotional intelligence plays an outsize role in this process, emerging as both a compass and a bridge in the leadership journey. It is the ability to navigate one's own emotions while tuning deeply into the feelings of others, creating resonance that fosters openness and connection. Leaders who cultivate emotional intelligence exhibit patience in adversity and humility in success, which paradoxically elevates their authority. Such leaders are not distant figures of command but are approachable, relatable, and deeply human. They listen actively rather than merely waiting to speak, validating concerns and ideas without judgment. This emotional attunement signals respect and builds psychological safety within teams and networks, encouraging innovation and mutual commitment. People instinctively gravitate toward leaders who can manage conflict with grace, comprehend unspoken cues, and maintain composure under pressure—all elements critical for trust to flourish.

Yet, emotional intelligence by itself is only part of the equation. Decisiveness is the forge where trust and influence are tempered into a reliable force. Leaders who hesitate excessively or waver under pressure quickly erode confidence among followers and partners. In contrast, those who combine empathy with clarity of vision and swift, informed decision-making inspire admiration and loyalty. This decisiveness should not be confused with impulsiveness; rather, it reflects a thoughtful yet bold mindset that weighs evidence and possible outcomes but does not become paralyzed by uncertainty. Every decision made as a leader sends a signal about your reliability and strategic foresight. Repeated patterns of sound decision-making reinforce your credibility, encouraging others to entrust you with opportunities that carry financial and relational rewards. Moreover, this decisiveness seeks momentum, generating progress and reinforcing an image of competence that magnifies influence even further.

Persuasive communication is the art form that knits together emotional intelligence and decisiveness into a coherent and compelling leadership presence. The way a leader conveys ideas, addresses concerns, and inspires action can either create walls or build bridges. Authenticity is the key that unlocks genuine persuasion — when words align with values and actions, the message resonates deeply and stands beyond superficial rhetoric. Master communicators craft narratives that not only inform but also evoke emotion and spark conviction, tapping into shared values and aspirations. They understand that influence is a two-way street and therefore strive for dialogue rather than monologue. Employing storytelling techniques that humanize abstract concepts, they make complex strategies accessible and motivate collective effort toward shared goals. This ability to communicate persuasively affects more than immediate transactions; it shapes culture, sets expectations, and crafts reputations that open doors to new financial prospects through partnerships and collaborations.

At the intersection of influence and trust lies consistency—the sometimes underrated but indispensable driver of leadership impact. The human psyche craves predictability in social interactions, especially when stakes are high, as in business and wealth-building endeavors. Leaders who consistently demonstrate reliability in their words and actions create a safe harbor for their teams, clients, and investors. This dependability builds a sturdy foundation of trustworthiness, encouraging others to take calculated risks and commit resources with confidence. Conversely, inconsistent behaviors breed skepticism, eroding influence over time. The commitment to consistency extends beyond face-to-face interactions to digital footprints and reputational capital. In today's hyper-connected world, leaders must vigilantly manage how they present themselves across all platforms, ensuring alignment between public persona and private values to maintain credibility.

Building influence and trust also involves mastering the delicate balance between humility and confidence, a dynamic tension that signals maturity and openness. Overconfidence can alienate and intimidate, while excessive humility risks underestimating one's own worth and diminishing authority. The artful leader projects a quiet, grounded presence — acknowledging limitations and inviting contributions from others while maintaining a clear sense of direction. This blend fosters inclusive leadership, where diverse perspectives are valued, and innovation thrives. Such environments attract high-caliber collaborators and partners who are essential for scaling financial success. Trustworthy leaders know when to step back and empower others, amplifying the collective intelligence and resilience of their networks. This distributive model of influence multiplies opportunities by creating a web of interdependent relationships where value flows freely in multiple directions.

The tangible benefits of influence and trust in the realm of financial freedom are manifold and profound. When a leader has cultivated a reputation for integrity and competence, they gain access to exclusive circles of capital and partnership. Investors and institutions, wary of risks in volatile markets, prefer aligning with individuals whose credibility can mitigate uncertainties. Similarly, business partners gravitate toward trustworthy collaborators because shared values and transparent communication drive synergy rather than friction. These connections often provide not only financial resources but also vital mentorship, knowledge exchange, and strategic alliances that accelerate growth. Moreover, a leader's influence can create ripple effects across industries and communities, attracting talent and customers who contribute to a sustainable ecosystem of prosperity. The ability to leverage one's network effectively hinges on the trust cultivated through consistent leadership behaviors, emotional intelligence, and persuasive communication.

This journey toward building influence and trust is neither linear nor effortless. It demands a relentless commitment to self-reflection and continual improvement. Leaders must be willing to face uncomfortable truths about their shortcomings and biases, correcting courses as needed. They invest time in understanding the evolving needs and motivations of their constituents, adjusting communication styles to resonate authentically. Failures and setbacks, inevitable along the way, provide critical learning opportunities if approached with humility and resilience. Ultimately, the leader who embraces this growth mindset enriches not only their personal wealth trajectory but also the communities they serve. In doing so, they transform influence from a transactional tool into a transformative force for purposeful and lasting impact.

As you embark on cultivating your own influence and trust, consider the intricate interplay of emotional intelligence, decisiveness, authenticity, consistency, and balanced humility. Reflect deeply on how these qualities express themselves in your daily interactions and decisions. Ask yourself whether your communication invites collaboration or resistance. Evaluate how your track record builds—or undermines—the confidence others place in you. Recognize that true influence is an emergent property of living your values visibly and intentionally. When honed, it empowers you not only to unlock new financial doors but to inspire a movement of wealth creation grounded in wisdom and character. In that space, leadership becomes a legacy, a beacon illuminating a path where financial freedom and purposeful growth walk hand in hand, opening possibilities far beyond individual gain toward collective prosperity.

Chapter 11: Entrepreneurship and Innovation

"Innovation distinguishes between a leader and a follower." — Steve Jobs

Key Takeaways

- Entrepreneurship creates wealth by solving problems.
- Innovation differentiates successful businesses.
- Every challenge presents an opportunity.
- Customer value drives business success.
- Calculated risks produce meaningful rewards.
- Persistence overcomes setbacks.
- Entrepreneurs create jobs and economic growth.

Entrepreneurial Mindset

Entrepreneurship, at its core, is less about the act of starting a business and more about embodying a mindset—a dynamic, tenacious way of perceiving the world that fuels innovation and propels individuals towards creating sustained value from opportunity. Cultivating an entrepreneurial mindset is akin to nurturing a fertile ground where resilience and creativity can flourish in tandem. It demands more than just the traditional traits often ascribed to entrepreneurs: passion, drive, and risk appetite. What distinguishes successful entrepreneurs is a deep-rooted ability to navigate uncertainty with optimism, to see challenges not as impediments but as invitations to problem-solve, and to maintain an unwavering commitment to iterative growth. This mindset begins with a fundamental orientation toward opportunity. Unlike passive observers, those with an entrepreneurial lens actively scan their environments, both local and global, seeking gaps, inefficiencies, or unmet needs that can be transformed into viable ventures. This opportunity recognition is often borne of acute curiosity and an openness to divergent ideas, where seemingly unrelated concepts are synthesized into breakthrough solutions. It is an acute sensitivity to the pulse of change—technological advancements, social trends, shifting consumer behaviors—that prime the entrepreneur to envision markets that don't yet exist or to reinvent existing frameworks with a fresh perspective.

Innovation, in this context, is not merely the creation of a new product or service but the application of creativity toward solving real problems with value-added solutions. The entrepreneurial mindset is fundamentally experimental. It embraces a rapid learning cycle, where hypotheses about products, customer preferences, and business models are tested through minimum viable products, pilot programs, or small-scale initiatives. Failure is recontextualized as feedback—a necessary step on the path to refinement and excellence. Here, resilience becomes the bedrock that supports this ongoing experimentation. Building resilience is more than enduring hardship; it's about developing psychological elasticity to rebound from setbacks, to maintain confidence during volatility, and to persist in the face of skepticism and obstacles. Entrepreneurs are often besieged by uncertainty—regulatory hurdles, capital constraints, marketplace competition—but it is the mindset of resilience that keeps them anchored, enabling strategic recalibration rather than surrender. This internal fortitude is frequently buttressed by a growth orientation, a belief that abilities and intelligence can be cultivated through effort, learning, and openness to feedback. This orientation encourages entrepreneurs to view every challenge as an opportunity to expand their capabilities and understanding, fostering adaptability in an ever-evolving economic landscape.

Risk management within the entrepreneurial framework takes a nuanced shape. It is not about eschewing risk altogether but about approaching risk analytically and strategically. Entrepreneurs hone the skill of discerning between calculated risks and reckless gambling, weighing variables, evaluating potential impacts, and preparing mitigation strategies to safeguard their ventures. This strategic agility involves a balancing act between boldness and prudence, where the entrepreneur navigates the tensions between seizing opportunities and protecting scarce resources. Importantly, risk is often diffused through the intelligent deployment of resources—diversifying customer bases, incremental scaling, leveraging partnerships, and using technology to reduce operational uncertainties. Aside from risk management is the crucial capability to scale ventures thoughtfully. Scaling, unlike a startup, demands shifting from the creative chaos of ideation into structured growth, where processes, systems, and leadership become paramount. The entrepreneurial mindset embraces scaling as a stage of evolution that requires foresight and systematization while retaining the innovative spirit that fueled initial success. Leaders with this mindset cultivate cultures of accountability, creativity, and continuous improvement within their organizations to sustain momentum. They understand that sustainable financial success is not merely a function of rapid expansion but of embedding resilience, adaptability, and customer-centricity into the organizational DNA.

This journey toward entrepreneurial mastery frequently involves an inner transformation as much as external action. Entrepreneurs cultivate an expansive self-awareness that enables them to manage stress, navigate ambiguity, and harness intrinsic motivation. This introspective dimension allows them to align their ventures with their core values and purpose, which amplifies their drive and authenticity. The entrepreneurial mindset also thrives on collaboration and community engagement. Recognizing that entrepreneurship is rarely a solitary endeavor, successful entrepreneurs seek diverse networks for advice, mentorship, and partnerships, understanding that collective intelligence often surpasses individual insight. They engage in active listening, empathy, and the building of trust—elements that foster authentic customer relationships and build sustainable competitive advantages. This relational orientation enhances their ability to identify unmet needs and co-create solutions with stakeholders.

Moreover, the entrepreneurial mindset is agile in its orientation toward technology and innovation ecosystems. Entrepreneurs who harness the power of digital tools and platforms—artificial intelligence, data analytics, automation—can amplify their creativity and operational efficiency. They use technology not just as a utility but as a strategic lever to redefine business models, access markets, and deepen customer engagement. This technological fluency infuses their ventures with scalability and flexibility, equipping them to respond swiftly to market changes and emerging opportunities. In an era of rapid disruption, the ability to integrate technology into the entrepreneurial process becomes a critical differentiator between fleeting ventures and enduring enterprises.

In essence, cultivating an entrepreneurial mindset is an immersive process that transcends business competencies. It is about fostering a resilient, creative, opportunity-focused perspective that embraces risk thoughtfully, innovates relentlessly, and scales sustainably. This mindset equips individuals to transform ambiguity into advantage, pioneering new value ecosystems that contribute meaningfully to economic growth and personal fulfillment. The richness of this mindset lies not only in the external successes it engenders but also in the profound personal transformation it demands—an evolution into a purposeful, agile, and visionary architect of both one's financial destiny and broader societal impact.

Chapter 12: Opportunity Recognition

"In the middle of difficulty lies opportunity." — Albert Einstein

Key Takeaways

- Opportunities exist where others see problems.
- Observation develops entrepreneurial insight.
- Preparation allows you to seize opportunities quickly.
- Markets need to create profitable businesses.
- Creativity enhances opportunity recognition.
- Continuous learning expands possibilities.
- Successful entrepreneurs remain alert to change.

Entrepreneurship begins with a spark—a moment of insight that reveals possibilities where others see obstacles, or a problem that demands a solution. This initial spark is not accidental; it is a cultivated mindset, a readiness to perceive potential opportunities in the fabric of everyday life. Opportunity recognition is, at its core, the ability to spot and evaluate business ideas that can transform from mere concepts into profitable ventures. It is the prism through which entrepreneurs view the world, filtering countless events and interactions through a lens shaped by curiosity, awareness, and strategic insight. This perceptual skill does not spring solely from intuition but emerges from a deliberate process of honing one's observational powers, gathering knowledge, and cultivating flexibility. When we understand how to recognize opportunities consciously, we gain the capacity to embark on ventures that are not only innovative but sustainable and aligned with the dynamics of the market and society.

The entrepreneurial mindset is fertile ground for opportunity recognition. It is characterized by a blend of optimism and realism, a willingness to challenge the status quo coupled with a disciplined approach to evaluating risks and rewards. Entrepreneurs see gaps—whether in products, services, systems, or experiences—and rather than retreat, they engage in thoughtful inquiry. They ask questions that disrupt complacency: Why does this problem exist? Who is most affected? How have others tried to solve it, and why have those attempts fallen short? They develop empathy toward the end user, gaining intimate understanding of their pain points and desires. This deep human-centered perspective is often the birthplace of innovative ideas, guiding entrepreneurs to create offerings that resonate authentically with their intended audience.

Innovation is the lifeblood of opportunity. Yet, innovation should not be mistaken for simply inventing something radically new. It often means adapting, recombining, or improving existing elements to meet emerging needs or untapping markets. Opportunity recognition involves the creative recombination of known components to forge unique value propositions. This re-engineering can harness technology, new business models, or shifts in cultural trends. For instance, the rise of the sharing economy was not about inventing new goods but about transforming ownership and access paradigms. Recognizing such shifts requires acute awareness of social movements, economic currents, and technological trajectories. Entrepreneurs who maintain an open mind toward interdisciplinary insights and who remain attuned to evolving customer behaviors are often the first to spot these inflection points where opportunity and timing converge.

Evaluating potential opportunities demands rigorous analysis beyond enthusiasm. A brilliant idea, unmoored from realities of market demand, capital requirements, competitive landscape, and operational feasibility, risks becoming a costly misadventure. Entrepreneurs refine their judgments by balancing data-driven insights with intuitive patterns discerned from experience. This process may involve market research, competitor analysis, or pilot testing. It also requires honest reflection on personal strengths and limitations, resource availability, and timing. A compelling opportunity aligns well with the entrepreneur's competencies and context, reducing unnecessary exposure to fatal risks. Effective risk management emerges from this alignment, where uncertainties are acknowledged but approached with strategic safeguards—such as minimum viable products, phased investments, or partnerships—that modulate exposure while enabling learning and adaptation.

Risk, however, should not paralyze the entrepreneur; instead, it is an inescapable aspect to be skillfully navigated. Successful opportunity recognition understands risk as a dynamic variable—one influenced by the entrepreneur's ability to acquire knowledge, build networks, and respond flexibly to feedback. Here, mindset shifts again, as risk transforms from a foe to a calculated component of exploration and growth. Entrepreneurs who develop resilience and a tolerance for ambiguity are better equipped to iterate on their ideas, learning continuously from failures without capitulating fear. This iterative agility is particularly essential in a world of rapid change, where initial assumptions can be quickly invalidated, and adaptability becomes a competitive advantage.

Scaling—the process of expanding a business beyond its initial scope—is the natural progression once an opportunity transforms into a tangible venture with proven value. Scaling requires a distinct set of skills and strategic vision, reminding us that opportunity recognition does not end at inception but extends through growth phases. Entrepreneurs must develop systematic processes, delegate effectively, and optimize resource allocation to sustain momentum. Recognizing when and how to scale involves reading signals from market traction, operational capacity, and organizational readiness. Premature scaling risks diluting focus and straining resources, while delayed scaling may forfeit market leadership. This delicate balance underscores the importance of a continuous learning loop—where success at one phase informs preparation for the next. Entrepreneurs who master this continuum from opportunity recognition to scaling create ventures not only profitable in the short term but robust and adaptable for lasting impact.

In practical terms, opportunity recognition can be strengthened through deliberate techniques and habits. One method is environmental scanning—a disciplined observation of trends, technologies, consumer behavior, and regulatory shifts. Entrepreneurs who allocate time regularly to this scanning develop mental maps of potential disruptions and niches. They immerse themselves in diverse contexts, attend conferences, engage with various communities, and absorb insights from fields beyond their own expertise. This cross-pollination fuels creativity and uncovers intersections where unique problems and solutions reside. Another technique is scenario planning, which involves envisioning multiple possible futures and assessing how current trends could evolve. This forward-thinking exercise broadens perspective and helps identify opportunities that might emerge under different conditions, enabling more informed and flexible strategies.

Network cultivation also plays a critical role in recognizing opportunities. Human connections provide real-time signals and alternative viewpoints that can illuminate blind spots. Entrepreneurs who actively nurture relationships with mentors, peers, customers, and even competitors gain access to knowledge flows and collaborative potential. These social resources amplify the ability to surface ideas and validate assumptions. Moreover, meaningful engagement with communities ensures that opportunities are grounded in real needs, avoiding speculative or disconnected ventures. Networking is thus not merely transactional but deeply relational, embedding opportunity recognition within a social fabric that reinforces both innovation and accountability.

Storytelling and narrative framing are often overlooked but powerful tools for opportunity evaluation. Entrepreneurs who can articulate the vision and impact of their ideas compellingly are better prepared to attract support, whether through investors, partners, or customers. Crafting these narratives requires clarity about the problem, the unique solution offered, and the value created. This communicative skill also doubles as an internal filter, forcing entrepreneurs to distill their concepts and test the coherence and appeal of their propositions. The ability to inspire is a strategic asset, converting abstract opportunities into tangible movements that galvanize resources and drive momentum.

The digital revolution and the rise of artificial intelligence have expanded the landscape of opportunity recognition dramatically. AI tools now allow entrepreneurs to access and analyze vast datasets, uncover patterns, forecast trends, and personalize offerings in unprecedented ways. Harnessing these technologies can dramatically enhance decision-making by providing evidence-based insights, reducing uncertainty, and accelerating innovation cycles. However, embracing technology also demands vigilance about ethical considerations and unintended consequences, ensuring that profit-seeking does not sacrifice values or social responsibility. Entrepreneurs who integrate advanced analytics with human judgment and ethical mindfulness position themselves to discover and cultivate opportunities that are not only financially rewarding but socially constructive.

In addition to external techniques, internal reflection and mindset cultivation remain central to opportunity recognition. Entrepreneurs benefit from cultivating mindfulness and cognitive flexibility, which enable them to question assumptions and explore alternatives creatively. Regular self-reflection helps identify biases or fears that may cloud judgment, opening space for bolder and more nuanced perspectives. This mental openness complements learning agility, the commitment to continuously acquire new knowledge and skills—and the willingness to pivot when new evidence emerges. Opportunity recognition is thus a dynamic dance of exploration and analysis, creativity and discipline, intuition and rigor.

Ultimately, opportunity recognition is a multifaceted process that integrates mindset transformation, thoughtful evaluation, and strategic scaling. It demands a holistic approach that balances optimism with realism, creativity with critical analysis, and vision with execution. Entrepreneurs who develop this skill not only unlock profitable business ideas but contribute to ecosystems of innovation and impact. They act as connectors—linking unmet needs with practical solutions, translating complexity into clarity, and converting ideas into value. Through deliberate cultivation of perception, resilience, and strategic thinking, opportunity recognition becomes less a chance occurrence and more a replicable and teachable competency, a cornerstone of lasting financial success and meaningful entrepreneurial legacy.

Chapter 13: Risk and Reward Management

"Risk comes from not knowing what you're doing."
— Warren Buffett

Key Takeaways

- Every investment involves risk.
- Managing risk is more important than avoiding it.
- Diversification protects wealth.
- Informed decisions reduce unnecessary losses.
- Evaluate both potential gains and consequences.
- Balance confidence with caution.
- Smart risk-taking builds long-term prosperity.

Entrepreneurship is, at its core, a dance with uncertainty. It is a realm where visionary ideas meet the unpredictable currents of real-world markets and human behavior. To step confidently into this arena, one must develop a nuanced understanding of risk and reward, not as opposing forces but as intertwined elements essential to informed decision-making. The mindset of the entrepreneur is pivotal in this balance, requiring more than just courage or intuition; it demands a disciplined approach to evaluating possibilities, harnessing innovation, and managing the inevitability of setbacks with resilience and strategic foresight.

Risk, in the entrepreneurial context, is multifaceted. It is not merely the possibility of financial loss but encompasses operational challenges, market fluctuations, competitive pressures, and even the personal toll of uncertainty and stress. Entrepreneurs often face the unpredictable nature of launching a new product, entering an untested market, or scaling a venture amid shifting economic landscapes. Yet, risk is not something to be feared or avoided indiscriminately. Instead, it should be understood through a lens of calculated assessment. This means systematically identifying potential threats and opportunities, quantifying their probable impact, and developing strategies to mitigate adverse effects without stifling innovative potential.

To balance risk with reward effectively, entrepreneurs must cultivate an analytical yet adaptive mindset. This involves rigorous market research to uncover unmet needs or inefficiencies that an innovative solution can address. Innovation, in this sense, serves as the engine of entrepreneurial success, but it must be grounded in reality. An imaginative idea without feasibility is a beautifully crafted illusion. The truly successful entrepreneur is adept at validating concepts through pilot programs, customer feedback loops, and agile iterations that refine the product or service while minimizing wasted resources. This approach minimizes exposure to unnecessary risk and maximizes the probability of market acceptance and growth.

Moreover, understanding opportunity cost is vital. Every decision to invest time, capital, or resources in one path inherently means forgoing alternative ventures. Savvy entrepreneurs constantly weigh these trade-offs, assessing which opportunities align best with their long-term vision and capacity for execution. This strategic prioritization requires a clear grasp of one's strengths, market dynamics, and emerging trends. Sometimes the highest rewards are found not in the most obvious or popular sectors but in niche markets where innovative disruption can yield disproportionate benefits. Such opportunities often come cloaked in ambiguity and require a willingness to embrace unconventional thinking without succumbing to reckless speculation.

Risk management, therefore, is not the antithesis of entrepreneurial ambition but rather its safeguard. Entrepreneurs employ a variety of tools to navigate this landscape. Financial instruments, such as diversified investment portfolios or phased funding rounds, help spread exposure and provide flexibility. Insurance mechanisms can shield ventures from catastrophic failures, and legal protections safeguard intellectual property. On the operational side, building robust networks and partnerships can distribute responsibilities and reinforce resilience against external shocks. This collective approach mitigates personal and business vulnerabilities, enabling entrepreneurs to leap toward innovation with a safety net beneath them.

Scaling a venture introduces a new dimension of risk and reward. Early-stage startups often focus on product development and market fit, but scaling demands mastering operational efficiency, expanding teams, and navigating complex supply chains or regulatory environments. Here, risks grow as the stakes rise; small miscalculations can multiply into significant losses. Sustainable financial success hinges on the entrepreneur's ability to balance aggressive growth ambitions with prudent resource allocation. This includes investing in leadership development, establishing scalable business processes, and maintaining a culture that embraces continuous learning and adaptability.

Importantly, risk and reward management is deeply psychological as well as strategic. The entrepreneur's mindset must reconcile the paradox of boldness and caution, optimism and realism. Overconfidence can lead to overextension and burnout, while excessive risk aversion may result in missed opportunities and stagnation. Developing emotional intelligence is critical to navigating this spectrum. Entrepreneurs must remain grounded in facts and data while cultivating the resilience to persist through failures. Every setback should be viewed as a learning moment rather than a defeat, each obstacle an invitation to refine strategy rather than abandon the quest.

This psychological balance is further influenced by the entrepreneur's personal values and purpose. When risk-taking is aligned with a mission that transcends mere profit—whether to innovate for social good, empower communities, or create lasting impact—it imbues the journey with meaning that sustains motivation and sharpens decision-making. Purpose-driven entrepreneurship transforms risk from a source of anxiety into a catalyst for intentional action, guiding entrepreneurs to prioritize long-term rewards over short-term gains and fostering sustainable business models.

In today's rapidly evolving landscape, technology plays an indispensable role in enhancing risk and reward management. Advanced data analytics, artificial intelligence, and machine learning tools empower entrepreneurs to forecast trends, simulate scenarios, and optimize operations with unprecedented precision. By harnessing these technologies, entrepreneurs can identify subtle market signals and emerging consumer preferences that human intuition alone might miss. This digital foresight supports more informed risk assessments and enables dynamic adjustments to business strategies in near real-time, significantly increasing the probability of success.

Furthermore, the democratization of technology breaks down traditional barriers to entry, allowing entrepreneurs to pilot innovations with relatively low capital investment compared to previous decades. Cloud computing, digital marketing platforms, and online marketplaces provide scalable avenues for testing and expanding business models. This reduces the initial financial risk and accelerates feedback cycles, empowering entrepreneurs to iterate rapidly and pivot as necessary. However, reliance on technology also introduces new risks related to cybersecurity, data privacy, and digital disruption, necessitating sophisticated risk management frameworks tailored to the digital age.

Strategic partnerships amplify both risk mitigation and reward potential. Collaborating with industry experts, investors, or complementary businesses allows entrepreneurs to share knowledge, resources, and networks. These alliances can accelerate product development, open new distribution channels, and enhance credibility in highly competitive markets. Yet, partnerships also entail relational risks—misaligned goals, communication breakdowns, or conflicts of interest can derail ventures. Therefore, successful entrepreneurs approach partnerships with rigorous due diligence, clear agreements, and continuous relationship management, understanding that trust and mutual benefit from the bedrock of enduring collaborations.

An essential aspect of risk and reward management is the cultivation of a resilient financial foundation. Entrepreneurs must maintain mindfulness over cash flow, liquidity, and capital structure, ensuring sufficient buffers to weather inevitable downturns. This fiscal discipline requires meticulous budgeting, scenario planning, and contingency reserves. It also demands transparency with stakeholders and the flexibility to secure additional funding when strategic opportunities arise or unforeseen challenges emerge. The ability to balance debt and equity financing, negotiate favorable terms, and time funding rounds strategically profoundly impacts a venture's capacity to sustain growth and navigate turbulent periods.

Moreover, incorporating feedback mechanisms from customers, team members, and mentors creates a dynamic feedback loop that enhances decision-making quality. Entrepreneurial ventures thrive when learning is embedded in the organizational culture. This openness to external input reduces cognitive biases that often lead to overlooked risks or inflated expectations. Listening to diverse perspectives enables entrepreneurs to anticipate market shifts, identify operational weaknesses, and innovate solutions proactively. In this way, the entrepreneurial journey is less a solitary gamble and more a networked pursuit of collective wisdom applied to risk and reward management.

Ethical considerations also shape how entrepreneurs approach risks and rewards. Responsible entrepreneurship integrates social and environmental impacts into decision-making processes. Entrepreneurs who prioritize ethical standards foster trust among customers, employees, and communities—a critical intangible asset that can differentiate brands and create lasting competitive advantages. Conversely, neglecting ethics in the quest for rapid rewards can lead to reputational damage, legal consequences, and market rejection, all of which represent significant risks. Therefore, sustainable wealth involves embedding integrity and corporate social responsibility at the heart of entrepreneurial strategies.

The narrative of entrepreneurship is often glamorized as a swift rise to wealth, but the reality is far more complex and nuanced. True mastery of risk and reward management emerges from a deep appreciation of the entrepreneurial process as iterative and adaptive. Success is rarely linear; it is punctuated by pivots, recalibrations, and continuous refinement. This journey demands not only strategic acumen but a persistent commitment to growth, learning, and self-awareness.

Entrepreneurs who master this balance develop ventures capable of weathering storms, seizing emergent opportunities, and creating enduring value—in essence, building financial freedom both for themselves and their broader ecosystems.

Looking ahead, the evolving global economy—with its blend of technological disruption, shifting consumer behaviors, and environmental uncertainties—will place even greater emphasis on sophisticated risk and reward management. Entrepreneurs equipped with a comprehensive framework that integrates mindset, innovation, strategic planning, technology adoption, and ethical stewardship will be better positioned to navigate complexity and unlock transformative potential. In essence, the art of balancing risk and reward transforms entrepreneurship from a mere career choice into a purposeful journey of value creation and legacy building.

In conclusion, embracing the interplay of risk and reward is a defining hallmark of entrepreneurial success. By cultivating a mindset that marries boldness with prudence, fostering innovation grounded in verification, deploying strategic risk management tools, and aligning efforts with personal and societal values, entrepreneurs can make informed decisions that propel sustainable financial growth. This balanced approach empowers them to turn uncertainty into opportunity, challenges into catalysts, and ideas into impactful enterprises—ultimately crafting not just wealth, but a meaningful legacy that transcends financial metrics.

Chapter 14:
Scaling and Growth Strategies

"Growth is never by mere chance; it is the result of forces working together." — James Cash Penney

Key Takeaways

- Sustainable growth requires planning.
- Systems support business expansion.
- Delegation increases productivity.
- Innovation sustains competitive advantage.
- Financial discipline fuels growth.
- Measure performance consistently.
- Growth should be intentional and strategic.

Entrepreneurship, at its core, is a journey of transformation—not just of ideas into tangible businesses, but of mindset into resilience, vision, and adaptability. Scaling and growth strategies embody this transformation, acting as the vital engine that propels enterprises beyond fledgling initiatives into robust, sustainable entities capable of generating significant financial returns. The process of scaling a business is not a mere transactional step; it is an intricate dance of identifying the right opportunities, cultivating relentless innovation, managing risks with shrewd foresight, and enacting strategic decisions that multiply value without diluting the essence of the venture. To understand and master scaling is to embrace the mindset of expansive entrepreneurship—a mindset that simultaneously dreams big and acts with disciplined precision.

One cannot discuss scaling without first engaging deeply with the entrepreneurial mindset that fuels it. This mindset is marked by a conscious shift from focusing on day-to-day survival to centering attention on long-term vision and possibility. Successful entrepreneurs who scale effectively perceive growth not as an accidental byproduct but as the intentional outcome of calculated decisions, continual learning, and relentless adaptation. They internalize a fundamental truth: growth requires discomfort. As business scales, the challenges morph from simple operational issues to complex systemic concerns that demand higher-level thinking, robust processes, and fluid leadership. The entrepreneurial psyche pivots from reactive problem-solving to proactive opportunity seeking. It becomes an evolving mental framework where failure is deconstructed not as defeat but as data—a vital source of insight informing iterative innovation.

Identifying opportunities for growth involves more than spotting trends or chasing market gaps. It demands a nuanced understanding of the market ecosystem, customer sentiments, emerging technologies, and competitive landscapes. The most scalable ventures are those that align deeply with unmet or latent customer needs, intersecting demand with innovation in unique ways. Here, empathy becomes a strategic asset; truly understanding the pain points and aspirations of potential customers enables entrepreneurs to design offerings that resonate on a profound level. Moreover, it is crucial to recognize that opportunities are dynamic and multi-dimensional. What appears as a niche today can evolve into a mainstream market tomorrow. The entrepreneur attuned to this dynamic nature consistently scans the horizon, scanning regulatory shifts, cultural transformations, and technological breakthroughs, always poised to pivot or expand accordingly.

Innovation in the context of scaling is often misunderstood as solely invention or the creation of new products. While groundbreaking ideas certainly play a role, innovation within scaling primarily revolves around refining and reinventing business models, processes, and customer experiences to unlock exponential value. This type of innovation is systemic and integrative; it challenges the status quo, dismantles limiting dogmas, and reconstructs the venture's architecture for enhanced efficiency, market penetration, and responsiveness. For instance, companies that pioneer innovative distribution channels or leverage data analytics to personalize customer engagement often access scaling trajectories unavailable to competitors anchored in traditional methods. Innovation also breathes life into the culture of a growing corporation, fostering an environment where teams are empowered to experiment, take calculated risks, and rapidly iterate, fostering agility, which is essential in navigating the turbulent waters of expansion.

Risk management in scaling ventures is a critical yet complex dimension that intertwines closely with innovation and opportunity recognition. Scaling inherently escalates exposure to operational, financial, market, and strategic risks. Entrepreneurs must therefore cultivate a dual lens—seeing both the promise of growth and the shadows of potential pitfalls. Effective risk management transcends the simplistic notion of avoidance. Instead, it is the art of informed risk-taking, where entrepreneurs meticulously evaluate the trade-offs between risk and reward, establish robust contingency plans, and diversify their approaches to mitigate vulnerabilities. This includes prudent financial stewardship, such as maintaining liquidity to weather unforeseen disruptions or strategically leveraging external investments without surrendering control. It also involves risk diversification across products, markets, and partnerships to buffer potential shocks. Founders who master this balancing act exhibit not only courage but disciplined prudence, setting the stage for enduring scalability.

Once the entrepreneurial mindset is cultivated, opportunities identified, innovation ingrained, and risks managed, the scaling process itself unfolds as a multilayered strategic endeavor. At its essence, scaling is about expanding the business infrastructure—systems, people, processes, and technology—to handle increasing demand and complexity without sacrificing quality or customer satisfaction. One foundational approach to scaling is establishing repeatable operational processes that reduce reliance on individual heroics and foster consistent delivery of value. Scaling breaks the bottleneck of limited capacity by automating or optimizing critical workflows, enabling the business to serve more customers more efficiently. In the modern economy, this often involves integrating sophisticated technologies that streamline supply chains, customer relationship management, and financial reporting. Beyond internal systems, scaling demands expanding human capital through strategic recruitment, leadership development, and a culture aligned with evolving organizational goals.

A pivotal strategic dimension of scaling lies in market expansion—whether geographically, demographically, or through diversification of product or service lines. Entrepreneurs seeking to grow their ventures must rigorously assess which markets hold the highest potential for sustainable returns and fit the company's core competencies and brand values. Market expansion is a balancing act between chasing growth and maintaining operational excellence. Entering new markets carries the complexities of unfamiliar regulations, cultural nuances, competitive dynamics, and customer behaviors. Successful scaling ventures often engage in meticulous market research and alliances with local partners who bring crucial contextual knowledge and credibility. Strategic partnerships and collaborations frequently accelerate scaling, opening doors to new distribution channels, technologies, and customer segments while sharing risks and investments.

Financial strategy during scaling is equally consequential and merits deliberate attention. Businesses that scale without a well-articulated financing plan frequently succumb to cash flow crises or become captive to unfavorable funding terms. Growth capital, be it from personal savings, debt instruments, venture capital, or strategic investors, must be deployed with transparency, accountability, and a clear roadmap for generating returns. Smart entrepreneurs align their financial strategy with the growth stages of their venture—early scaling might prioritize reinvestment of profits and bootstrap funding, while later stages may call for structured rounds of capital infusion aimed at rapid market domination or innovation acceleration. Equally important is managing cost structures and margins during growth to ensure that increased sales volume translates into proportional or enhanced profitability rather than undue expense escalation.

Leadership emerges as perhaps the most transformational element in scaling a business. The founder or leadership team's ability to evolve is paramount; what drives a startup's initial spark is often insufficient to sustain a larger, more complex organization. Leaders must embrace adaptability, emotional intelligence, and the aptitude to delegate and empower others effectively. Building a strong leadership bench and succession plan prevents bottlenecks and supports sustained momentum. Furthermore, cultivation of an inclusive and purpose-driven corporate culture aligns employees with the mission and energizes collective effort. Leadership in scaling ventures is not about command and control but about nurturing a shared vision, fostering innovation at all levels, and maintaining relentless focus on customer value delivery.

Technology plays an indispensable role in contemporary scaling strategies, serving as the enabler that breaks numerous traditional barriers to growth. Digital transformation—from cloud computing and data analytics to artificial intelligence and automation—equips businesses with tools to enhance decision-making quality, customer insights, operational efficiency, and scalability. For example, leveraging AI-powered predictive analytics allows companies to forecast demand accurately, personalize marketing campaigns, and optimize inventory management, reducing costs and increasing revenue potential. Furthermore, adopting e-commerce platforms or digital marketing broadens reach with relatively lower incremental costs compared to brick-and-mortar expansion. The pace of technological evolution demands entrepreneurs remain vigilant, continuously educating themselves and their teams to harness emerging tools ethically and effectively within their scaling strategies.

In practical terms, scaling does not follow a linear script; it demands iterative cycles of planning, execution, assessment, and refinement. Businesses must develop robust feedback loops that capture real-time data on performance metrics and customer satisfaction to make rapid adjustments. Flexibility remains a competitive advantage, allowing ventures to reallocate resources or pivot when original assumptions no longer hold. Scaling also requires a patient, long-term orientation and a willingness to invest time and resources into foundational capabilities that may not yield immediate profits but establish durable competitive advantages. Patience is critical to withstand the turbulence often accompanying rapid growth phases, including market fluctuations, operational growing pains, and shifts in team dynamics.

Many entrepreneurs find that scaling necessitates relinquishing some degree of control and embracing external expertise. Bringing in advisors, consultants, or professional managers can infuse fresh perspectives and specialized skills essential for robust growth. The transition from a founder-led solo operation to a professionally managed organization is a common and necessary evolution to sustain scaling momentum. Effectively navigating this transition entails clear communication of vision and values, deliberate governance structures, and incentives aligned to foster an ownership mentality among team members.

Ultimately, the goal of scaling and growth strategies transcends merely increasing revenues or market share is about building a sustainable architecture for financial success and impact that endures beyond the individual founder. Sustainable scalability integrates economic goals with ethical considerations, social responsibility, and alignment with personal and organizational purpose. Entrepreneurs who embed values into their growth blueprint secure the trust of customers, employees, investors, and communities, which in turn creates a resilient foundation resistant to market shocks or reputational risks.

Sustainability in scaling is interconnected with scalability; growth fueled by fleeting trends or unsound practices often leads to collapse. Instead, embedding discipline in financial stewardship, continuous innovation, strong leadership, and customer-centricity ensures that growth is both profitable and responsible. Scaling becomes a journey of creating a compounding value virtuous cycle where resources generated through growth are reinvested into talent development, technological advancement, and community engagement, catalyzing further growth in an upward spiral.

In reflection, the journey of scaling and growth is an intricate tapestry woven with threads of mindset, opportunity, innovation, risk mastery, strategic execution, leadership, and technology. Entrepreneurs who internalize this interconnected framework equip themselves not only to expand their business operations but also to create meaningful, lasting wealth. They move beyond the transactional metrics of financial gain to envision wealth as multidimensional—encompassing legacy, purpose, and contribution. Scaling, therefore, is not an end but a continuum of deliberate choices and transformations that cultivate freedom and impact, echoing far beyond the confines of profit and into the realm of enduring fulfillment.

Chapter 15: Building Human Capital

"The greatest asset of a company is its people." — Jorge Paulo Lemann

Key Takeaways

- People are an organization's greatest asset.
- Investing in education increases future earnings.
- Leadership develops talent.
- Collaboration strengthens performance.
- Knowledge compounds over time.
- Strong teams achieve greater results.
- Human capital drives economic development.

The Power of Mentorship

In the vast landscape of wealth-building, where countless strategies and approaches compete for attention, the power of mentorship stands out as an unrivaled catalyst for acceleration and transformation. The journey toward financial freedom can often feel like navigating uncharted waters — complicated, intimidating, and prone to setbacks. Yet, nestled within this voyage lies a profound truth: no one reaches the heights of success entirely alone.

The relationships we cultivate, especially those forged with mentors, can serve as pivotal fulcrums, dramatically shifting our trajectory with insights, encouragement, and access to networks otherwise out of reach. Mentorship, therefore, is not merely a supplementary aid but a cornerstone upon which enduring financial growth and personal evolution are built.

When we consider mentorship, it is vital to transcend the casual notion of simply having someone older or more experienced offer advice. True mentorship embodies a dynamic, reciprocal relationship where wisdom passes through a sustained bond of trust, vulnerability, and commitment. The mentor acts as both a guide and a mirror, helping the mentee to see not only external opportunities but also internal limitations that might obstruct progress. Such relationships often reveal hidden strengths and expose blind spots, fostering a level of self-awareness that textbooks and seminars rarely achieve. With mentorship, the mentee gains a nuanced navigation system calibrated to their specific ambitions, personality, and challenges, enabling them to make smarter decisions, avoid common pitfalls, and seize rare chances.

The immediacy of learning from mentors dramatically condenses the timeline for growth. Where countless hours might otherwise be wasted on trial and error, mentorship offers curated experiences and distilled knowledge that can leapfrog a person over years of stumbling in the dark. Consider the subtleties imbued in a mentor's guidance: nuanced financial advice tailored to current market conditions, behavioral insights about managing risk, or strategic introductions to influential networks. These elements converge into a potent blend of intellectual capital that a mentee would find difficult to accumulate independently. It's not just about what you know, but who you learn it from and how you apply that knowledge in real time. Mentors reveal the invisible architecture behind successful ventures, enabling mentees to perceive patterns, trends, and leverage points that accelerate their accent exponentially.

Building this mentorship relationship requires intentionality and vulnerability. It is an investment of time, energy, and authenticity, where a mentee must be willing to listen deeply, embrace constructive criticism, and pursue growth relentlessly. Many aspiring individuals underutilize mentorship potential because they underestimate the depth of commitment required or they shy away from exposing their insecurities. Yet, these are precisely the openings through which mentors can make the most profound impact. When mentees cultivate a posture of learning humility, seeking feedback instead of validation, they unlock doors to breakthroughs that propel not only their financial futures but also their personal maturity. This attitude transforms the mentorship dynamic into a powerful engine for exponential progress rather than a passive relationship.

Furthermore, mentorship enriches one's social capital — a subtle but potent form of wealth that is often overlooked in conventional financial discussions. Relationships built through mentorship frequently extend into larger networks that provide access to partnerships, opportunities, and resources otherwise inaccessible. Social capital operates like an invisible currency, where trust and rapport create reciprocal obligations and enable the circulation of opportunities within these networks. Entrepreneurs and professionals who actively engage in mentor-mentee ecosystems often find themselves invited into inner circles of innovation, collaboration, and influence. This access confers a unique advantage and can manifest in invitations to investment deals, strategic collaborations, or high-impact knowledge exchanges that foster wealth creation in ways more traditional approaches cannot replicate.

The power of mentorship is also magnified by its ability to model character and discipline alongside skill and knowledge. Successful mentors do more than impart financial tactics; they embody the virtues—integrity, resilience, patience—that underpin lasting prosperity. Observing how mentors navigate adversity, handle ethical dilemmas, and balance ambition with responsibility provides mentees with real-life templates for sustainable success. Such modeling transcends theoretical understanding and imprints practical wisdom embedded in lived experience. This transfer of tacit knowledge has a ripple effect, shaping not just what mentees do but fundamentally who they become as leaders, entrepreneurs, and stewards of wealth.

In practical terms, finding a mentor calls for strategic thinking and authentic engagement rather than passive hope. Mentors can appear in various forms—from seasoned industry veterans and thought leaders to peers with complementary strengths. The key lies in identifying individuals whose experiences resonate with your aspirations and who are willing to invest time in your growth. Building these connections may involve stepping out of comfort zones, attending industry events, joining mastermind groups, or leveraging digital platforms where knowledge exchange thrives. Once contact is made, nurturing the relationship entails showing genuine appreciation, demonstrating progress, and seeking ways to reciprocate value, forging bonds that transcend transactional interactions.

Another crucial dimension of mentorship is its adaptability over career stages and financial milestones. Early in one's journey, a mentor might focus on cultivating foundational skills, decision-making frameworks, and mindset shifts that set the stage for upward mobility. As the mentee matures, the relationship can evolve into sophisticated strategic dialogues about scaling businesses, diversifying portfolios, navigating leadership challenges, or pioneering innovation. This longitudinal nature of mentorship ensures continuous alignment with the mentee's growth trajectory, maintaining relevance and maximizing impact over time. Importantly, successful mentorships often evolve into lasting partnerships or friendships, creating enduring support systems that anchor the mentee's professional and financial ecosystem.

Moreover, in today's rapidly changing economic climate, mentorship takes on renewed significance. Emerging technologies, shifting market dynamics, and global interconnectedness introduce complexities that can overwhelm even seasoned investors and entrepreneurs. Mentors provide invaluable contextual interpretation of these trends, helping mentees discern noise from signal, adapt strategies fluidly, and capitalize on disruptive innovations. In this sense, mentorship is a dynamic dialogue that blends timeless principles with cutting-edge insights, empowering individuals to remain agile and forward-thinking. When technology transforms industries overnight, the mentor's role as a compass guiding prudent adaptation becomes a critical asset.

The transformative impact of mentorship can be observed in countless stories of extraordinary success grounded in collaborative wisdom. Consider the entrepreneur who, through mentoring relationships, avoids costly missteps in scaling a startup, or the professional who transitions into financial independence by applying nuanced tax strategies shared by a trusted guide. These narratives underscore mentorship's role as a multiplier, where the combined effect of experience, guidance, and network access accelerates outcomes far beyond solo effort. The ripple effect also extends beyond individual gains, as mentees often pay forward lessons learned, nurturing subsequent generations and perpetuating a cycle of empowerment and wealth expansion.

Mentorship's role in fostering resilience and perseverance cannot be overstated. Along the rollercoaster of wealth-building, setbacks, failures, and doubts are inevitable. In moments of discouragement, mentors serve as anchors, reminding mentees of their potential and reframing obstacles as opportunities for growth. This psychological reinforcement combats isolation and fuels motivation, helping individuals to sustain disciplined habits and strategic focus even in turbulent times. The encouragement and accountability inherent in mentorship relationships create protective buffers against burnout and impulsive decisions that jeopardize long-term wealth.

Finally, the holistic nature of mentorship extends beyond financial metrics to encompass personal fulfillment and purpose alignment. Wealth devoid of meaning can be hollow, but mentors can provoke deep reflection on how financial goals intersect with life's broader ambitions. Through mentorship, individuals are encouraged not only to measure their success in numbers but to evaluate the impact, legacy, and values embedded in their wealth creation. This alignment fosters a form of prosperity that nourishes the soul and spurs more meaningful contributions to communities and causes. By integrating character development with strategic acumen, mentorship instills a balanced approach to wealth—one that elevates both individual well-being and shared progress.

In sum, the power of mentorship lies in its capacity to provide personalized guidance, accelerate learning, expand social capital, and model the intangible qualities essential to enduring success. As individuals seek to build financial freedom through skill-building, strategy, and smart decisions, mentorship emerges as an indispensable lever — transforming aspirations into achievable realities. It shifts the paradigm from isolated effort to collaborative growth, from temporary victories to sustainable wealth grounded in wisdom and purposeful relationships. Embracing mentorship as a central component of one's wealth equation is not merely advisable; it is a profound investment in a future defined by opportunity, resilience, and impact.

Chapter 16: Networking for Financial Gains

"Success in business is through people, through people, through people." — Richard Branson

Key Takeaways

- Strategic relationships create financial opportunities.
- Collaboration multiplies success.
- Mentorships accelerate growth.
- Professional communities expand knowledge.
- Reciprocity strengthens networks.
- Relationships often produce opportunities unavailable through formal channels.
- Invest in people as intentionally as investments.

In the intricate tapestry of wealth building, networking emerges not merely as a supplementary activity but as a fundamental pillar that can profoundly influence financial trajectories. The practice of connecting with others transcends superficial interactions; it becomes a strategic art form where relationships serve as conduits of opportunity, knowledge, and influence. To understand the true power of networking for financial gains, one must first recognize that wealth creation is rarely an isolated endeavor. Rather, it thrives in ecosystems where individuals support, challenge, and propel one another toward higher ambitions. By investing time, energy, and genuine interest into cultivating strategic relationships, you unlock a reservoir of social capital that often proves to be as valuable as financial capital itself. These relationships introduce you to new perspectives, markets, partnerships, and funding sources that might remain inaccessible when operating solo. Far beyond the cliché of exchanging business cards, effective networking imbues your journey with leverage, creating a multiplier effect on your efforts and resources.

The initial step in harnessing networking for financial growth is reimagining what relationships mean in a professional and personal context. Instead of transactional encounters aimed at immediate gain, consider building a web of connections anchored in mutual respect, authenticity, and long-term value creation. This mindset shift is crucial because relationships grounded solely in self-interest tend to wither or collapse when circumstances change. Enduring networks flourish when nurtured with empathy, openness, and a sincere desire to contribute to others' successes. When you approach networking with an authentic attitude, people become more willing to share insights, opportunities, and mentorship, which are often reserved for trusted allies rather than casual contacts. The richness of these human connections cannot be overstated; they become bridges to new ecosystems that can accelerate financial accumulation in myriad ways.

Mentorship holds a unique and transformative place within the spectrum of networking. A mentor is more than a guide; they are a living repository of experience, wisdom, and hard-earned lessons. Engaging mentors in your professional journey acts as a catalyst to fast-track your learning curve, navigate pitfalls, and seize opportunities with greater confidence and clarity. Unlike formal education or self-study, mentorship delivers personalized insight, tailored feedback, and encouragement grounded in real-world complexity. A great mentor introduces you to their own networks, effectively extending your reach and credibility. This introduction is priceless because it comes with an implied endorsement, facilitating trust and engagement within new circles. Over time, the counsel and connections derived from mentorship serve as a foundation upon which strategic decisions and ventures can flourish, transforming knowledge into tangible financial outcomes.

However, attracting and maintaining such high-caliber mentoring relationships demands patience, humility, and reciprocity. It requires you to invest in the mentor with your time, effort, and openness to critique, showing that their guidance is valued and impactful.

Successful mentees are those who also bring value to the table, whether through fresh ideas, assistance in projects, or simply by amplifying the mentor's legacy through respectful partnership. Through this symbiotic interaction, relationships evolve from one-dimensional teacher-student dynamics into robust alliances that continue to bear fruit long after formal mentorship phases conclude.

Beyond mentorship, the broader concept of social capital encompasses the full spectrum of your personal and professional networks. Social capital is less about the number of contacts and more about the quality, diversity, and depth of interactions within that network. When carefully curated, a diverse social capital portfolio grants access to varying industries, cultures, expertise, and viewpoints; factors that dramatically expand your creative and strategic possibilities. For instance, a finance professional may benefit from connections in technology, marketing, or policymaking, each offering distinct insights or gatekeeping roles in different domains. Moreover, relationships that bridge social, economic, or geographical divides create bridges spanning knowledge and opportunity gaps, enabling you to identify and capitalize on emerging trends or underserved markets that competitors might overlook.

Maintaining and enhancing this network requires deliberate, ongoing effort. Passive networking—waiting for opportunities to knock or only reaching out when in need—rarely results in deep, productive connections. Instead, active engagement through continuous communication, shared experiences, and collaborative endeavors strengthen bonds. Simple but meaningful actions such as celebrating others' achievements, helping without expecting immediate return, and inviting peers to co-create ventures or learning experiences foster goodwill and mutual investment. Social capital, therefore, behaves similarly to financial capital; it appreciates with consistent care and depreciates if neglected. A strong network buffers challenge and opens doors precisely when you need support most new job, investment opportunities, or strategic partnerships.

The digital era has revolutionized traditional networking paradigms, adding new layers of complexity and opportunity. Online platforms like LinkedIn, industry-specific forums, and virtual conferences remove geographical barriers and democratize access to influential circles once reserved for a select few. However, the sheer volume of connections introduced by digital means can dilute relationship quality if not managed thoughtfully. Instead of amassing hundreds or thousands of shallow contacts, prioritize meaningful engagement with select individuals, cultivating trust through regular, insightful interaction. Personalized messages, thoughtful content sharing, and participation in niche groups where you can contribute uniquely enhance your digital social capital. The goal is to transform digital acquaintances into substantial relationships that support your financial ambitions with the same depth and commitment as in-person connections.

Moreover, networking for financial gains is inseparable from the cultivation of emotional intelligence and interpersonal skills. The ability to listen deeply, empathize, communicate clearly, and manage social nuances distinguishes individuals who convert connections into opportunities from those who fail to do so. It is essential to read beyond surface-level greetings or polite conversations to discern shared values, unspoken needs, and latent synergies that thrive beneath the surface of casual interaction. Developing genuine curiosity about others—not just their titles but their dreams, challenges, and motivations—builds rapport that transcends business facades and nurtures trust. In many cases, deals or collaborations materialize based on this foundational human understanding long before formal negotiations or contracts appear on the table.

Another dimension of networking involves strategic alliances and collaborative ventures that multiply financial returns. Strategic alliances emerge when two or more parties combine strengths, resources, and networks to achieve objectives neither could efficiently attain alone.

For example, a startup might partner with an established corporation to access distribution channels, while the corporation benefits from the startup's innovation. These alliances are often born from well-maintained networks where trust has been nurtured and aligned interests identified. Cultivating such partnerships requires foresight to recognize complementary capabilities, patience to negotiate terms reflecting mutual benefit, and integrity to maintain commitments over time. The financial gains from these collaborations are often exponential because synergy creates value far exceeding the sum of individual efforts.

It is equally important to appreciate that networking is not a one-way street. The most enduring relationships flourish on an ethic of generosity and contribution. When you adopt a mindset geared toward giving—whether sharing knowledge, endorsing others, making introductions, or providing encouragement—you build a reputation as a reliable and valuable network node. This reputation, in turn, begets invitations, referrals, and goodwill that open new avenues for financial growth. Paradoxically, by focusing less on what you can extract and more on what you can invest in others, you activate a virtuous cycle where resources flow back to you in unexpected and often richly rewarding ways.

Consider the anecdote of an entrepreneur who, early in her career, prioritized helping peers succeed without immediate reciprocation. Over time, these actions built a dense ecosystem of allies who championed her ventures, introduced her to investors, and advised her at critical junctures. The key to this success was not random generosity but strategic altruism; she sought to empower others whose values and goals aligned with her own, creating a network founded on shared vision and trustworthiness. This approach exemplifies how networking is less about opportunistic hustling and more about fostering interconnected communities that uplift collective and individual prosperity.

In practical terms, integrating networking as a core pillar of financial strategy demands developing a multi-dimensional approach. This involves setting clear objectives—such as learning about new markets, finding partners, or exploring investment opportunities—while remaining adaptable to serendipitous connections that broaden horizons unexpectedly. Formal networking events, while valuable, represent only one facet of relationship-building. Informal settings such as shared hobbies, volunteer work, or intellectual circles often yield deeper, more resilient connections because they arise from authentic shared interests rather than agenda-driven contexts.

Interview exercises and reflective questions amplify networking success by increasing self-awareness and strategic intent. Ask yourself, for example, which relationships have contributed most to your growth and why. What qualities do these connections share? Where are the gaps in your network in terms of expertise, diversity, or influence? How can you add value to your existing contacts? Proactively answering such questions refines your networking tactics, ensuring that efforts align with long-term financial goals rather than short-term gratifications. Furthermore, it encourages continuous learning and self-improvement, traits inseparable from successful wealth architects.

It is also imperative to navigate networking with a keen sense of ethics and discernment. In a world rife with opportunism and superficial exchanges, maintaining integrity safeguards your reputation and ensures enduring relationships. Transparency about intentions, honoring commitments, and respecting boundaries foster trust—a non-negotiable currency in any prosperous network. Ethical networking resonates with the book's foundational theme of building wealth through wisdom, character, and discipline. It mitigates risks such as exploitation, burnout, and cynicism, which can derail both individual success and collective progress. Ultimately, the quality and sustainability of your relationships reflect the values and principles you uphold.

As you refine your networking prowess, do not underestimate the power of storytelling and personal branding in attracting connections and opportunities. Humans connect deeply through narratives that resonate emotionally and intellectually. Sharing your journey, aspirations, and lessons authentically create affinity and positions you as a relatable and trustworthy individual. When others understand your purpose and character, they are more likely to champion your endeavors, offer guidance, or provide introductions that align with your goals. This narrative clarity also equips you to identify and engage with those who share similar values or complementary ambitions, enhancing the network's coherence and functionality.

In the final analysis, networking for financial gains is a dynamic, evolving discipline that intertwines interpersonal skills, strategic vision, ethical commitment, and continuous engagement. It is less about quantity and more about cultivating rich, reciprocal relationships that augment your human and financial capital. As you weave networks built on trust, generosity, and aligned purpose, you create a fertile ground for opportunities to emerge organically and compound over time. The power of relationships to open doors, amplify influence, and accelerate success cannot be overstated. Through deliberate and heartfelt networking, you transform your journey toward financial freedom from a solitary climb into a collective ascent supported by a vibrant community of allies, mentors, and partners. This collective strength becomes one of the most reliable equations in the grand formula of lasting wealth.

Chapter 17: Collaborative Wealth Building

"If you want to go fast, go alone. If you want to go far, go together." — African Proverb

Key Takeaways

- Wealth grows faster through collaboration.
- Partnerships combine complementary strengths.
- Shared goals create mutual success.
- Trust is essential for successful collaboration.
- Clear communication prevents conflict.
- Collective knowledge improves decision-making.
- Collaboration creates larger opportunities than working alone.

We live in an age where the adage “no man is an island” is truer and more crucial than ever, especially when it comes to building wealth. The journey to financial freedom, while deeply personal, is rarely a solitary endeavor. Collaborative wealth building transcends mere networking or transactional relationships; it is a deliberate and ongoing investment in partnerships, alliances, and community ties that weave together to multiply opportunities and resources. At its core, this approach recognizes that wealth—broadly defined as financial capital, human capital, social capital, and intellectual capital—is most effectively grown when shared, exchanged, and nurtured through relationships founded on trust, mutual respect, and aligned objectives. This is not about parasitic connections or exploiting others for gain but about creating ecosystems of support where each participant contributes, learns, and benefits in a sustained, virtuous cycle.

The power of collaboration in wealth building fundamentally lies in leverage. When you align yourself with the right people—mentors who have traveled the path ahead, peers who challenge and inspire, partners who bring complementary strengths—your efforts compound exponentially. Imagine a skilled entrepreneur who understands product development but lacks marketing savvy. By forming a partnership with a marketing expert who recognizes the value of the product and shares the vision, both parties enhance their chances of success far beyond what solitary endeavor could achieve. This is partnership by design, not by default. It demands intentionality, clarity of purpose, and a willingness to share control and rewards. Collaborative wealth invites us to shift from a zero-sum mindset, where one person's gain is another's loss, to an abundance mentality where the pie grows bigger and everyone at the table benefits.

This process begins with social capital—the goodwill, trust, and networks you cultivate through authentic human connection. Unlike financial capital, which is quantifiable and often finite, social capital's value is dynamic and expansive, growing with each meaningful interaction and investment of time. Building social capital demands vulnerability, active listening, generosity, and consistency. It requires showing genuine interest in others' goals, ambitions, and challenges. When you nurture relationships with sincerity, you create a foundation where collaboration can flourish naturally. These relationships act as conduits for knowledge exchange, introductions to new opportunities, and supportive environments for growth. Over time, your social capital serves as a reservoir of potentially to be tapped when opportunities arise or challenges emerge.

Mentorship stands as one of the most valuable forms of collaborative wealth building. A mentor provides guidance, wisdom, and feedback that can save years of trial and error. Engaging with mentors means investing in relationships where experience meets aspiration. This dynamic is not unidirectional; while mentees gain knowledge and perspective, mentors often find renewed purpose and fresh ideas to invigorate their own endeavors. Learning from those who have navigated the complexities of wealth creation, how to overcome setbacks, avoid pitfalls, and recognize unseen opportunities—offers immense leverage. Importantly, mentorship stretches beyond just financial advice; it encompasses leadership, emotional intelligence, and strategic thinking. Such holistic growth equips individuals not only to build wealth but to sustain it and perpetuate it responsibly.

Beyond individual mentors, cultivating alliances with like-minded entrepreneurs and professionals can establish a network of mutual support and innovation. These alliances often foster environments where collaborative problem-solving and co-creation occur. When individuals pool their unique skills and resources, they trigger creative synergies that generate ideas and ventures no one could have realized alone. In today's rapidly shifting economic landscape, where technology disrupts, consumer behaviors evolve, and markets fluctuate, having a trusted circle of collaborators offers resilience. This community can provide diverse viewpoints that guard against groupthink, offer constructive critique, and accelerate adaptive strategies. Moreover, joint ventures or strategic partnerships can open access to new markets, capital sources, and customer bases, amplifying growth potential exponentially.

However, harnessing the power of collaboration for wealth creation requires more than assembling a network; it demands cultivating high-quality relationships based on integrity, transparency, and shared values. Trust becomes the currency of these alliances. Without trust, collaborations crumbled under suspicion and misaligned incentives. Leaders who exemplify character and commitment attract partners eager to engage in long-term wealth building rather than quick gains. Transparency in intentions, decision-making, and financial matters further solidifies trust and ensures accountability. Shared values align participants' visions, solidifying common purpose and easing conflicts. In this sense, collaborative wealth creation is an ethical endeavor as much as a financial strategy; it respects the dignity and aspirations of all involved, fostering prosperity that is inclusive and sustainable.

Investment in others through mentorship or partnership should be viewed as a strategic asset, not merely a philanthropic gesture. When you support someone else's growth with time, knowledge, or access, you are effectively sowing seeds for future harvests. People remember those who elevate their trajectory, and they often reciprocate that goodwill when new opportunities arise. This reciprocal support creates a feedback loop of abundance, where everyone benefits from collective progress. In the ecosystem of wealth building, "giving" is thus inseparable from "receiving." The mindset shift from isolated competition to collaborative creation is transformational; it dissolves scarcity fears and invites innovative thinking about how resources and success are shared and multiplied.

In a practical sense, implementing collaborative wealth building starts with investing intentional time and energy into deepening relationships rather than accumulating superficial contacts. It involves moving from casual networking events to forming mastermind groups, regular check-ins with mentors and peers, and creating forums for open exchange of ideas and challenges. Technology can be a facilitator here, connecting people across geographies and disciplines, but the core principles remain timeless: authenticity, generosity, and accountability. Those who master these relational dynamics find themselves at the crossroads of opportunity more often and with trusted allies by their side.

Moreover, as artificial intelligence and digital platforms evolve, collaborative wealth building is gaining new dimensions. Technology enables more efficient matchmaking of complementary skills and resources, breaking down traditional barriers to collaboration. For instance, entrepreneurs today can engage in global partnerships with ease, collaborate on projects via virtual platforms, and leverage AI to analyze market trends in real-time. These tools amplify the scale and scope of wealth-building networks, making collaborations not only more diverse but also more data-driven and strategic. Yet no algorithm or platform can replace the human element of trust and shared vision that underpins successful alliances. Thus, while technology is a powerful enabler, the essence of collaborative wealth building remains deeply human.

Cultivating togetherness in wealth also invites us to reconsider the role of competition. Healthy competition pushes innovation and excellence, but when it devolves into cutthroat rivalry, it fractures communities and diminishes collective potential. Conversely, collaboration encourages a cooperative spirit where competitors may become allies, sharing insights or jointly tackling challenges—essentially creating what some refer to as "co-opetition." This phenomenon fosters a market environment where multiple players thrive because they leverage each other's strengths and expand the pie rather than fight over slices. Such environments attract talent, investment, and innovation, propelling all participants forward.

Reflecting on historical and contemporary examples, some of the world's most enduring wealth legacies have been built on collaborative foundations. Family businesses that span generations thrive when family members share aligned values, mentor the next generation, and create governance structures that support collective decision-making. Similarly, business ecosystems like Silicon Valley illustrate how dense networks of entrepreneurs, investors, advisors, and academics create fertile ground for continuous innovation and financial success. These communities thrive because collaboration is ingrained in their culture—not accidental or superficial but disciplined and intentional. This illustrates that collaborative wealth building is not idealistic fluff but a proven strategy that reliably delivers results when practiced with rigor and heart.

One of the most profound benefits of collaborative wealth building is its potential to democratize access to resources and opportunities. When individuals pool their expertise and capital, barriers that once limited participation in wealth creation can be lowered. Collaborative investment groups, cooperative ventures, and community development initiatives exemplify how collective efforts can unlock financial avenues for those traditionally excluded. This inclusive approach not only promotes social equity but also taps into a broader array of talents and ideas, enriching the creative and innovative potential of wealth ecosystems. It embodies a vision of wealth that elevates communities and creates shared prosperity rather than concentrating resources in isolated pockets.

Importantly, the longitudinal nature of collaborative wealth building means it often unfolds over years or decades, requiring patience, persistence, and stewardship. Quick, transactional wins can be satisfying, but durable wealth arises from ongoing cycles of investing in people, refining shared goals, navigating challenges, and celebrating collective achievements. This perspective reshapes how we view success—not as a solitary trophy but as the flourishing of all involved partners. It also encourages a mindset of stewardship, where the wealth created today embodies a responsibility to nurture and sustain the collaborative framework that made it possible, ensuring that future generations inherit a rich legacy—not just of assets but of relationships and wisdom.

For those embarking on this path, developing emotional intelligence is essential. Collaborative wealth building is deeply relational, involving nuanced communication, empathy, conflict resolution, and trust-building. The ability to understand others' perspectives, manage one's own emotions, and foster psychological safety can determine whether alliances thrive or falter. Leaders who hone these soft skills enable open dialogue, encourage diverse viewpoints, and build resilient partnerships capable of weathering disagreements or external shocks. This emotional dimension transforms collaborations from brittle arrangements into adaptive, dynamic networks where innovation and wealth creation continually evolve.

In sum, collaborative wealth building represents a paradigm shift in how we conceive of personal and collective financial success. It calls on us to recalibrate our approach from individualistic hustle toward interdependent growth, recognizing that the most profound financial breakthroughs often arise through connection and shared effort. By investing in relationships grounded in trust, learning from mentors, fostering alliances, and embracing technology as a tool rather than a substitute, we craft a rich tapestry of opportunities and support that propels us forward. This approach not only accelerates wealth accumulation but enriches our human experience, imbuing the pursuit of financial freedom with meaning, purpose, and enduring legacy. In embracing collaborative wealth building, we unlock the true potential of what it means to prosper—not just alone, but together.

Chapter 18:
Financial Capital and Investment Strategies

"Do not save what is left after spending, but spend what is left after saving." — Warren Buffett

Key Takeaways

- Capital should be allocated strategically.
- Diversification improves portfolio stability.
- Investments should align with financial objectives.
- Review your portfolio regularly.
- Patience is essential for investment success.
- Long-term thinking reduces emotional investing.
- Wealth grows through disciplined investing.

Diversification and Asset Allocation

In the complex and often unpredictable world of investing, diversification and asset allocation stand as pillars of prudent wealth management strategies. They form the foundational bedrock upon which investors, both novices and seasoned professionals, build resilient portfolios capable of weathering the inevitable storms of market volatility while simultaneously harnessing growth opportunities. At its core, diversification is the practice of spreading investments across various asset classes, sectors, geographies, and instruments to mitigate the risk of significant losses that can occur when an investor is overly concentrated in a single area. Conversely, asset allocation is the strategic process of determining the optimal proportion of these assets in a portfolio to align with individual risk tolerance, financial goals, and time horizons. Together, these approaches work symbiotically to balance risk and reward, creating a pathway for sustained wealth accumulation that is both intelligent and adaptive.

To truly grasp the power of diversification, one must first recognize the inherent uncertainty present in all investments. Markets fluctuate due to an array of factors—economic cycles, geopolitical tensions, technological disruptions, and investor sentiment, among others. No single asset or market segment is immune to downturns, no matter how promising it may appear on the surface. By allocating capital across different investments, the negative impact from one holding can often be offset by positive performance in another. For example, equities in emerging markets might falter due to regional instability, while developed markets may simultaneously rally due to robust economic policies and innovation. Similarly, bonds might provide steady interest income when stocks decline, adding a stabilizing effect to the portfolio's overall returns. This dynamic interplay between asset classes underscores the essence of diversification: to avoid placing all your financial eggs in one basket.

However, diversification is not merely about random dispersion of investments; it is a deliberate and thoughtful construct that requires comprehensive analysis and ongoing evaluation. Investors must look beyond superficial categorizations and delve into the correlations between asset returns, seeking combinations that do not move in tandem. Low or negatively correlated assets cement the foundation for reducing volatility and smoothing out returns over time. For instance, real estate might sometimes behave independently from commodities or stocks, offering unique value in turbulent times. Gold, traditionally viewed as a haven, is often appreciated during periods of inflation or currency devaluation, providing a critical hedge within a diversified structure. These interrelationships guide the intelligent assembly of a portfolio that minimizes risk without necessarily sacrificing potential growth.

Asset allocation builds upon the diversification framework by considering the investor's individual circumstances, aspirations, and behavioral tendencies. It answers the fundamental question: how much should be invested in stocks, bonds, cash equivalents, real estate, or alternative assets? This allocation is not static but evolves with the investor's life stage, financial goals, and prevailing economic conditions. A young investor with a long investment horizon and higher risk tolerance might allocate heavily toward equities or emerging asset classes that offer greater growth potential but come with volatility. They have time to ride out market fluctuations and capitalize on compounding returns. Conversely, an investor nearing retirement generally prioritizes capital preservation and income stability, leaning more toward fixed-income securities and less risky assets. Amid this balancing act, attention must also be paid to liquidity needs and tax implications, ensuring that the asset mix supports both flexibility and efficiency.

The science of asset allocation leans heavily on modern portfolio theory, which mathematically models risk and return to identify efficient portfolios. It emphasizes that a well-diversified portfolio aligned with an investor's risk profile can achieve higher returns for the same level of risk compared to non-diversified portfolios. Importantly, it challenges the outdated approach of chasing individual high-performing stocks or market timing, emphasizing instead the discipline of strategic allocation and periodic rebalancing. Rebalancing involves realigning the portfolio back to its intended asset mix after market movements cause drifts. This practice instills a buy-low-sell-high discipline: selling portions of overperforming assets and buying those that have underperformed, maintaining constant discipline against emotional impulses. Over time, rebalancing preserves the risk-return balance and enhances long-term performance, avoiding the dangers of "herding" behavior or panic selling.

Beyond traditional equities and fixed income, diversification and asset allocation now increasingly consider alternative investments and passive income streams as critical components of wealth-building. Alternative assets such as private equity, hedge funds, commodities, infrastructure, and real estate investment trusts (REITs) offer different return drivers and reduced correlation to public markets. They can act as shock absorbers during turbulence, infusing stability and enhancing portfolio diversification. Moreover, passive income through dividends, rental income, royalties, or interest can supplement capital gains, providing steady cash flows that reinforce financial security. The inclusion of such non-traditional income streams bolsters the ability to weather downturns without liquidating holdings prematurely, enabling investors to hold long-term positions integral to wealth accumulation.

The digital age has also revolutionized how diversification and asset allocation are implemented. Access to global markets, fractional investing, exchange-traded funds (ETFs), and robo-advisors has democratized portfolio construction, allowing even modest investors to build diversified, strategically allocated portfolios with minimal barriers. ETFs allow investors to buy baskets of securities spanning multiple sectors, geographies, and asset classes at remarkably low costs. This innovation reduces the complexity and transaction costs traditionally associated with building diversified portfolios, freeing investors to focus on portfolio design and outcomes rather than micro-managing individual stocks or bonds. Robo-advisors employ algorithm-driven strategies to recommend and maintain asset allocation aligned with risk profiles, automating rebalancing and tax-loss harvesting, further enhancing the efficiency and reliability of portfolio management.

The practice of diversification and asset allocation is also an ongoing journey requiring continuous education and adaptation to changing market environments. Investors must stay informed about macroeconomic trends, policy shifts, technological innovations, and shifts in consumer behavior, all of which influence asset class performance. For example, the rise of environmental, social, and governance (ESG) investing has created new asset categories and considerations, integrating ethical values into portfolio construction. The emergence of digital assets like cryptocurrencies challenges traditional portfolio paradigms, introducing new opportunities and risks. Smart investors approach these novel frontiers cautiously within a diversified framework that protects capital while capturing growth potential, always balancing innovation with proven principles.

Managing risks through diversification and asset allocation goes beyond market fluctuations and includes considerations such as inflation risk, interest rate risk, liquidity risk, and even psychological biases. Inflation erodes the purchasing power of money over time, and a portfolio heavily skewed toward cash or fixed-rate bonds might perform poorly in such an environment. Incorporating inflation-protected securities, real assets like commodities, or equities that tend to keep pace with inflation can safeguard wealth. Interest rate movements influence bond prices inversely; a spike in rates could reduce bond values, necessitating maturity laddering and duration management for risk control. Liquidity risk arises when an asset cannot be quickly sold without substantial loss in value, a crucial consideration especially for those nearing liquidity events. Diversifying across liquid and illiquid assets, while keeping sufficient reserves in accessible forms, strikes a balance between opportunity and availability.

Behavioral finance also plays a critical role in risk management within diversified portfolios. Emotional responses to market corrections—such as panic selling during downturns or exuberantly chasing bubbles—can derail even the most carefully constructed portfolio.

Diversification and asset allocation impose a disciplined structure that curbs impulsive decisions by setting clear boundaries and expectations. Investors are encouraged to develop patience and trust in the allocation strategy, seeing volatility as a natural and even beneficial aspect of investing rather than a trigger for fear. Reflective practices, including periodic review sessions and journaling investment experiences, help reinforce rational decision-making and emotional resilience. This psychological fortitude is essential for maintaining the course during challenging periods.

Moreover, a well-diversified, thoughtfully allocated portfolio supports broader financial planning objectives beyond mere wealth accumulation. It enables efficient tax management by strategically placing income-generating assets in taxable or tax-advantaged accounts to optimize after-tax returns. It allows for effective estate planning, ensuring that wealth transition across generations aligns with both financial goals and family values. It provides a foundation for financial independence by generating dependable income streams that reduce reliance on earned income, freeing individuals to pursue passions and purpose-oriented endeavors. In essence, diversification and asset allocation are not ends in themselves but instruments to empower holistic financial freedom rooted in stability, growth, and meaningful choice.

Navigating the multifaceted landscape of investment requires an integrated approach that harmonizes diversification and asset allocation with the evolving sophistication of markets and technologies. This means embracing both the timeless wisdom of spreading risk and tailoring portfolios to personal contexts, as well as leveraging modern tools that facilitate accessibility, automation, and informed decision-making. Whether through the broad exposure provided by international ETFs, the specialized niches of alternative investments, or the consistent income from real estate and dividend stocks, the overarching principle remains constant: no single investment or strategy holds all the answers. True financial resilience comes from the thoughtful orchestration of diverse assets aligned with a clear strategic vision and the agility to recalibrate as circumstances change.

Ultimately, the power of diversification and asset allocation lies in their capacity to turn uncertainty from a paralyzing foe into a manageable companion on the journey toward wealth creation. By respecting risk's presence and engineering portfolios that respond dynamically to change, investors craft financial ecosystems that are robust, adaptive, and growth oriented. This mindset transcends short-term speculation and aligns with a broader philosophy of disciplined, purposeful growth—a philosophy that is at the heart of sustained financial freedom. By weaving together the strands of diversification and asset allocation, investors don't merely chase returns; they craft enduring legacies of wealth built on the pillars of wisdom, patience, and strategic foresight.

Chapter 19: Creating Passive Income Streams

"If you don't find a way to make money while you sleep, you will work until you die." — Warren Buffett

Key Takeaways

- Passive income creates financial independence.
- Multiple income streams reduce financial risk.
- Assets generate income while you sleep.
- Invest in scalable opportunities.
- Automation increases efficiency.
- Passive income complements active earnings.
- Financial freedom depends on income beyond employment.

The concept of creating passive income streams often conjures images of earning money effortlessly, as if by magic. Yet, beneath this enticing promise lies a multifaceted process—one that demands careful planning, strategic investment, and deliberate cultivation of assets that can generate revenue with minimal ongoing effort. The allure of passive income is undeniable, particularly when one considers the transformative power it holds over one's relationship with money and time. Imagine waking up each morning knowing that your bank account has grown overnight, not solely because of the hours you put in, but because your money is working diligently on your behalf. This is the essence of passive income: establishing systems and investments that continue to yield returns long after the initial input of effort, freeing you to focus on other pursuits, be they personal passions, entrepreneurial ventures, or simply enjoying life's pleasures.

Yet, the journey to building sustainable passive income streams is neither a single leap nor a simple endeavor. It is a continuous process that requires intentional diversification to hedge against risks and maximize opportunities in a dynamic financial landscape. Diversification ensures that your income sources are not overly dependent on a single market, asset class, or economic condition. Just as a skilled orchestra requires varied instruments blending to create harmony, a resilient portfolio integrates diverse investments such as real estate, stocks, bonds, digital assets, and entrepreneurial ventures to harmonize income generation with both stability and growth. Through such a balanced composition, the volatility inherent in one area can be mitigated by the stability or upside potential of another, protecting your wealth accumulation journey from unexpected downturns.

Asset allocation becomes the linchpin in this strategic diversification, acting as the deliberate distribution of your capital across different categories to achieve an ideal risk-reward balance aligned with your financial goals, time horizon, and risk tolerance. This process is not static, but adaptive; it evolves as markets shift, your personal circumstances change, and new investment opportunities arise. The wisdom here lies in not putting all your eggs in one basket, but also in committing enough resources to each basket that they can truly thrive. For example, a higher allocation to dividend-paying stocks or income-focused mutual funds can create a steady cash flow, while a portion invested in growth-oriented assets builds capital appreciation potential. This balance is crucial, because a portfolio disproportionally weighted toward growth can carry significant volatility and risk losses that jeopardize your passive income streams, while overly conservative allocations may limit your income potential.

Among the most common and powerful passive income vehicles is real estate investing. When managed effectively, real estate can provide a dual benefit: asset appreciation over time and consistent rental income. The key is to start with careful market research—choosing locations with strong rental demand, good growth prospects, and favorable economic conditions. Yet, owning rental properties is not entirely passive—there is tenant management, maintenance, and administrative work involved. To truly embrace the passive nature, many investors employ property management companies or engage in partnerships which allow them to collect the income without the day-to-day operational headaches. Alternatively, Real Estate Investment Trusts (REITs) offer a more hands-off approach, allowing you to invest in portfolios of properties that generate income distributed as dividends. This method harnesses professional management and diversification benefits while requiring minimal ongoing effort on your part.

Dividend investing in the stock market is another foundational pillar for passive income creation. By selecting companies with strong fundamentals and a history of reliable dividend payouts, investors can cultivate a cash flow that compounds over time as dividends are reinvested. The beauty of dividend investing lies not just in income generation but in stability and predictability, crucial qualities for a sustainable passive income stream. However, discernment is vital—high dividend yields can sometimes indicate underlying company distress, while steady, increasing dividends often reflect sound corporate governance and resilient business models. Investing in dividend-focused exchange-traded funds (ETFs) or mutual funds can also provide a diversified exposure to high-quality dividend payers, reducing individual stock risk and creating a more balanced income portfolio.

A relatively newer frontier for passive income in the digital age involves monetizing assets through online platforms and technology. Creating digital products—such as e-books, courses, music, or software—once requires significant upfront work but can generate sales and royalties indefinitely. The scalability here is limitless, given the global reach and low distribution cost of the internet. Yet, success demands excellent content, market understanding, and strategic marketing to keep the sales flowing. Similarly, affiliate marketing, where you earn commissions by promoting other companies' products, or creating monetized online communities and subscription-based content, provide alternative streams with varying degrees of ongoing maintenance. Automation tools and outsourcing can reduce your daily involvement, nudging these ventures closer to true passivity over time.

Peer-to-peer lending and crowdfunding platforms have also emerged as innovative methods for passive income, where you lend money or invest in projects vetted by online marketplaces, earning interest or profit shares. While these options can diversify income streams further, they carry credit risk and liquidity considerations that require astute evaluation. Balancing the allure of higher returns with prudent risk management is an indispensable part of nurturing these novel income avenues.

Passive income streams, however, must not be mistaken for "set and forget" ventures. Even the most established investments require ongoing review and occasional recalibration. Economic cycles, regulatory environments, market dynamics, and technological advancements constantly reshape the landscape. The diligent investor maintains vigilance—tracking performance metrics, rebalancing portfolios, and adapting strategies—to ensure income streams remain robust and aligned with broader financial objectives. Discipline and education are crucial, empowering you to respond with agility rather than complacency. A passive income strategy thrives on this paradox: minimal active management in the daily sense, but ongoing active oversight in the broader perspective.

Equally important is managing financial risks to sustain wealth accumulation through these passive income streams. Risk management encompasses understanding the variability of returns, protecting assets from substantial losses, and securing income against interruptions. Diversification reduces concentration risk, but comprehensive insurance coverage, emergency cash reserves, and legal protections guard against unforeseen events like property damage, liability claims, or market crashes. Moreover, tax planning plays a fundamental role in preserving the net income generated. Intelligent structuring of investments, leveraging tax-advantaged accounts, and staying informed about changing tax laws can significantly elevate the real returns from passive income ventures.

Building passive income is as much a mental journey as it is a practical one. It demands a shift from the conventional trade-time-for-money mindset to a more expansive perspective that embraces patience, foresight, and resilience. True passive income streams are born from purposeful decisions made today—compounded by reinvestment, diversification, and vigilant stewardship—that bloom into sustainable wealth tomorrow. Rather than chasing fleeting trends or speculative jackpots, the discerning individual lays down steady bricks with diversified investments, carefully chosen assets, and prudent risk management to construct a sturdy financial foundation.

Throughout history, countless examples attest to the power of passive income in transforming lives. Visionaries who leveraged rental properties to fund early retirement, entrepreneurs who developed scalable digital products producing royalty income, or investors who built dividend portfolios that replaced their salary—all chose to prioritize income sources beyond active labor. These pioneers did not stumble upon fortune; they cultivated it with diligence, adaptability, and strategic insight. Their journeys remind us that passive income is not a myth but a disciplined practice that integrates knowledge, action, and persistence.

Ultimately, creating passive income streams is an art and science that requires synthesizing diverse financial instruments, technologies, and personal values into a coherent plan. It is a journey from dependency on active work to embracing financial freedom, where your assets act as tireless allies supporting your life's ambitions. As artificial intelligence and automation continue to advance, opportunities to refine and expand passive income will grow, offering even more innovative and accessible pathways. The truly successful wealth builders will welcome these changes with open arms, continuously learning and evolving their strategies to safeguard and amplify their income streams. The wealth equation is incomplete without a well-constructed, resilient passive income component—one that transforms effort into lasting freedom and empowers you to live purposefully without financial constraints holding you back.

Chapter 20: Risk Management in Investing

"Never test the depth of a river with both feet." — Warren Buffett

Key Takeaways

- Protect wealth before pursuing growth.
- Insurance is an important financial safeguard.
- Diversification minimizes investment losses.
- Market volatility is normal.
- Maintain an emergency reserve.
- Avoid emotional investing during market fluctuations.
- Review risk regularly as life circumstances change.

Risk management in investing transcends the mere intuition of avoiding loss; it is an intricate art and science that seeks to strategically protect capital while positioning oneself to benefit from market opportunities. It requires a multifaceted approach informed by deep understanding, disciplined execution, and an adaptable mindset. At its core, it involves recognizing that all investments carry inherent risks—whether market volatility, geopolitical instability, economic shifts, or the unique vulnerabilities of individual assets—and crafting a resilient portfolio designed not to eliminate risk, which is impossible, but to manage, mitigate, and balance it in a way that aligns with both one's financial goals and risk tolerance.

One of the foundational pillars of risk management is the concept of diversification. The age-old wisdom of not putting all eggs in one basket remains remarkably pertinent in today's complex financial ecosystem. Diversification works on the principle that different asset classes, industries, and geographic regions react differently to various economic forces, and thus, when combined thoughtfully, they can reduce overall portfolio volatility. The skill lies in selecting a blend of assets whose performance is not highly correlated. For instance, equities may flourish during economic expansions, while bonds often provide stability during downturns; real estate can act as an inflation hedge; commodities might respond differently to currency fluctuations and global supply constraints. By spreading investments across stocks, bonds, real estate, commodities, and even alternative assets like private equity or cryptocurrencies, an investor can create a buffer against severe losses tied to any one market movement or sector collapse. This strategy requires continuous evaluation as correlations between assets can evolve over time due to shifting economic landscapes or structural changes in markets.

Another vital technique in risk management relates to asset allocation, which is the deliberate distribution of capital across different asset classes based on an investor's objectives, time horizon, and risk appetite. Asset allocation is a dynamic exercise, not a static event, demanding periodic reassessment in response to changing personal circumstances and evolving market conditions. It's important to understand that asset allocation can often be more impactful on long-term portfolio outcomes than selecting individual securities. A well-constructed allocation plan layered with built-in risk controls—such as caps on the percentage in high-volatility assets or floors in safer investments—helps prevent emotional decision-making during turbulent markets. For example, younger investors with longer horizons may allocate more to equities for growth, balancing with fixed income and cash equivalents as they approach retirement. The principle of 'time diversification' suggests that exposure to more aggressive investments can be moderated by the ability to weather short-term fluctuations over a longer timeframe. However, this does not guarantee immunity from risk and underscores the pertinence of recalibrating allocations in response to shifts in market valuations, interest rates, and personal financial goals.

Approaching risk management also involves embracing the discipline of regular portfolio rebalancing. This process realigns investments back to their original or desired target allocations after market movements create drift. Without rebalancing, a portfolio's risk profile may inadvertently shift: a surge in equity prices could outweigh risk exposure beyond acceptable limits, while a drop in safer assets may reduce means to cushion downturns. Rebalancing, though occasionally uncomfortable—often requiring selling winners and buying laggards—grounds an investor in a prudent framework that curtails the excesses of greed and fear. It's a vital guardrail that enforces discipline and ensures the portfolio remains aligned with predetermined strategies rather than capitulating to short-term market sentiments. This not only mitigates risk but positions the portfolio for sustained growth, emphasizing the balance between protecting capital and capturing opportunities.

Integral to managing risk is the expert use of passive income streams, which serve as financial cushions that reduce reliance on capital gains alone. Passive income, derived from dividends, interest, rental income, royalties, or business cash flows, provides a steadier inflow of funds that can be reinvested or used for personal expenses, thereby reducing the urge to liquidate investments unfavorably during market downturns. This stability enhances an investor's psychological resilience, allowing more measured responses to market volatility. Moreover, establishing diversified passive income streams mitigates business or industry-specific risks, further solidifying the financial foundation. The beauty of passive income lies in its compounding potential and the way it can supplement traditional portfolios, enhancing both liquidity and financial flexibility, which are crucial elements in long-term risk management.

Beyond diversification, asset allocation, rebalancing, and passive income, sophisticated investors deploy a variety of strategic risk management tools and techniques, informed by quantitative and qualitative analysis. Hedging strategies, for example, use financial derivatives such as options, futures, and swaps to protect against downside risks. Put options, which grant the holder the right to sell an asset at a predetermined price, serve as insurance policies against price declines. Futures contracts can lock in prices or hedge commodity and currency exposures. Swaps can mitigate interest rate or credit risks. While these instruments offer powerful means to control exposure, they require a high degree of understanding and discipline, as misuse or overreliance can magnify losses. Successful hedging balances cost against benefit, aiming not to eliminate risk altogether but to reduce its impact to tolerable levels.

Risk management also entails rigorous due diligence and continual monitoring of investments and market conditions. Understanding the underlying fundamentals of assets, including business models, competitive positions, debt structures, and management quality, enables investors to better judge the likelihood and severity of potential losses. This qualitative insight complements quantitative metrics like volatility, beta, value at risk (VaR), and scenario analyses, fostering a more comprehensive risk assessment. Investors must stay attuned to macroeconomic indicators, geopolitical developments, regulatory changes, and technological disruptions that can rapidly alter market trajectories. Employing real-time data analytics and technological tools, including AI-driven predictive modeling, can enhance early detection of shifts, enabling proactive rather than reactive risk management.

Psychological factors profoundly influence risk management efficacy. Behavioral biases such as overconfidence, loss aversion, herd behavior, and recency bias often undermine rational decision-making, leading investors to take excessive risks or panic prematurely. Cultivating emotional discipline and a long-term perspective is therefore paramount. Successful investors develop mental frameworks that embrace uncertainty and oscillations in market conditions as normal rather than exceptional. They view downturns as opportunities for disciplined purchasing rather than triggers for fear-induced selling. This mindset aligns tightly with the principle of risk tolerance—the degree of variability in investment returns that an individual is willing to withstand without emotional turmoil—and risk capacity, or the financial ability to endure losses without jeopardizing fundamental goals. Both must be carefully assessed and respected in constructing risk management protocols.

Insurance products represent another layer of protection within a comprehensive risk management strategy, particularly for non-investment risks that can impact financial stability and, indirectly, investment portfolios. Health, disability, life, property, and liability insurance safeguard against unexpected financial shocks that could force premature liquidation of assets or derail long-term plans. Though insurance premiums represent a cost, they are investments in preserving capital and maintaining integrity of the wealth-building journey.

Liquidity management is a critical aspect often overlooked in traditional investment strategies but paramount in protecting capital. Liquidity—the ease with which assets can be converted into cash without significant loss—ensures investors can meet short-term needs or capitalize on opportunities without distress selling. Maintaining an appropriate portion of portfolios in cash or highly liquid securities serves as a buffer during market disruptions, enabling measured responses rather than forced reactions. This liquidity reserve is a cornerstone of disciplined risk management, preserving optionality and reducing vulnerability to margin calls or sudden funding needs.

An often-underrated element of risk management is the setting of clear investment rules and exit strategies. Before entering an investment, defining criteria for holding, adding, or selling can prevent emotional indecision or impulsive actions. Stop-loss orders, for example, automatically trigger sales once an asset falls to a certain price, limiting potential losses. Trailing stops adjusting dynamically with market appreciation to protect gains while allowing further upside. Conversely, profit-taking strategies lock in returns rather than chasing endlessly higher prices subject to inevitable reversals. These predetermined boundaries imbue the investor with control amidst market unpredictability, transforming risk from a nebulous threat into a controllable element of decision-making.

The evolving landscape of financial technology offers novel avenues for advancing risk management. Artificial intelligence and machine learning algorithms exponentially enhance data analysis, pattern recognition, and predictive capabilities. These technologies enable real-time risk assessment at unprecedented scales and granularity, accommodating complex portfolios spanning international markets and multiple asset classes. Robo-advisors democratize access to systematic portfolio management with embedded risk controls, making sophisticated strategies accessible even to non-expert investors. Blockchain technology enhances transparency and security in transactions, reducing operational risks. However, as investors increasingly integrate technology, they must remain vigilant about cyber risks and data integrity, adding new dimensions to risk management frameworks.

Environmental, social, and governance (ESG) factors represent another critical frontier in modern risk evaluation. Investments in companies with poor environmental practices or governance inconsistencies may face regulatory penalties, reputational damage, or long-term sustainability challenges, all of which translate into financial risks. Incorporating ESG analysis into investment decisions not only aligns portfolios with ethical considerations but also mitigates risks that traditional financial metrics might overlook. This dimension underscores the holistic nature of risk that extends beyond markets into the broader societal context.

In the broader arc of wealth creation, risk management is inseparable from the philosophy of prudent stewardship and intentional growth. It demands humility to acknowledge uncertainty and limitations of predictive powers, coupled with courage to embrace calculated risk as the price of opportunity. It is not a passive shield but an active, ongoing process of learning, adapting, and refining strategies in tandem with life's changing rhythms and external environments. The goal is to craft a resilient financial foundation that withstands shocks while nurturing growth—a balance between defense and offense.

To embrace risk management effectively, investors must view loss not as failure but as an essential instructor on the path to mastery. Every setback is a lesson revealing vulnerabilities, testing discipline and resolve, and catalyzing improved frameworks. A successful investor evolves not only in technical skill but in character—cultivating patience, fortitude, and clarity of purpose. This inner wealth fortifies external wealth against storms.

In summary, risk management in investing is a sophisticated endeavor rooted in diversification, thoughtful asset allocation, disciplined rebalancing, and the creation of multiple passive income streams. It leverages advanced financial instruments, qualitative and quantitative analyses, and emerging technologies to mitigate exposure while capitalizing on growth opportunities. It demands a deep understanding of personal risk tolerance and capacity, psychological discipline, and preparedness through insurance and liquidity buffers. By integrating these elements into a coherent, dynamic strategy, investors can protect their capital and enhance the probability of sustained wealth accumulation. Far from being an afterthought, risk management is the very equation that transforms uncertainty into opportunity and preserves the journey toward financial freedom.

Chapter 21:
Technology and Wealth: The AI Revolution

"The best way to predict the future is to invent it." — Alan Kay

Key Takeaways

- Artificial intelligence is transforming wealth creation.
- Technology increases productivity and efficiency.
- AI creates new investment opportunities.
- Digital skills improve career prospects.
- Innovation rewards adaptable individuals.
- Use technology ethically and strategically.
- The future belongs to continuous learners.

AI in Financial Decision-Making

In the rapidly evolving landscape of finance, artificial intelligence has emerged as a transformative force that reshapes the way individuals and institutions approach financial decision-making. At its core, AI offers the remarkable ability to analyze vast oceans of data with precision and speed unmatched by human cognition alone. This capability opens the doors to a new era where investing and budgeting—two pillars of personal and professional financial planning—can be executed with extraordinary intelligence, foresight, and efficiency. AI's role is not merely supplementary; it is catalytic, unleashing innovative methodologies for wealth creation that transcend traditional frameworks. What distinguishes AI-driven financial decision-making is its proficiency in recognizing patterns from the noise, generating actionable insights, and anticipating shifts in markets and behaviors that often elude even the most astute human analysts. The convergence of machine learning, natural language processing, and advanced algorithms equips AI systems to sift through historical data, current market conditions, global economic indicators, and even social sentiment to craft strategies that optimize outcomes while managing risk.

In the realm of smarter investments, AI empowers investors by providing analytical rigor across diverse asset classes, enabling more informed and timely choices. Unlike conventional investment analysis, where decisions hinge largely on human intuition and static models, AI can dynamically adjust its recommendations based on real-time data streams. For instance, robo-advisors, a popular application of AI in personal finance, automate portfolio management by continuously evaluating an individual's risk tolerance, financial goals, and market conditions. These platforms offer personalized investment strategies, balancing asset allocation with rebalancing tactics that respond instantly to market volatility. Beyond automation, AI enables advanced predictive modeling, identifying underpriced securities or emerging sector trends by uncovering subtle correlations within complex datasets. This ability deeply enhances the investment research process, allowing investors to access insights previously reserved for high-level institutional players equipped with vast resources. Moreover, AI-driven sentiment analysis can gauge the broader market mood by scanning news outlets, social media, and global events, providing an additional layer of intelligence that enriches decision-making. Investors who harness these tools move beyond reactive trading toward proactive strategy formulation, enhancing portfolio resilience and maximizing growth potential.

When it comes to budgeting, AI's contribution is equally profound and transformative. Traditional budgeting techniques often falter under the weight of human error, inconsistent tracking, and delayed responsiveness. AI-powered budgeting tools function by continuously monitoring an individual's expenditures, income flows, and behavioral spending patterns through integration with banking and financial accounts. These tools offer real-time financial visibility that is personalized and predictive, flagging areas where expense management can be improved and suggesting adjustments that align spending with long-term financial goals. By automating expense categorization and forecasting cash flow, AI eliminates tedious manual bookkeeping tasks and mitigates the risk of oversight or miscalculation, thereby fostering greater financial discipline and clarity. Beyond mere tracking, AI systems employ behavioral analytics to unlock deeper insights into moments of impulsivity or recurring cost drivers, offering tailored recommendations that encourage smarter spending habits. This level of customization not only improves day-to-day financial management but also cultivates a heightened sense of financial awareness and control. Over time, individuals gain the ability to anticipate future financial scenarios, such as changes in income or unexpected expenses, with actionable roadmaps that maintain budgetary harmony amid life's uncertainties.

The power of AI extends far beyond automation and analytics; it actively unleashes new wealth-building opportunities by democratizing access to sophisticated financial tools. Previously, such resources were accessible primarily to elite investors with specialized knowledge or capital. AI levels this playing field, offering user-friendly platforms that empower people from varying economic backgrounds to optimize their financial futures. For example, automated trading algorithms customized for retail investors allow participation in markets with precision timing and risk control previously unattainable without extensive expertise. Similarly, AI-powered credit scoring systems evaluate alternative data points beyond traditional credit reports, enabling individuals with limited histories to access loans or financial products that fuel entrepreneurial ventures or asset accumulation. Emerging platforms harness AI to curate micro-investment strategies, fractional asset ownership, or decentralized finance applications, making financial participation inclusive and scalable. Through this technological empowerment, AI not only augments existing wealth-building pathways but creates entirely new ones that recognize diverse financial realities and ambitions. These disruptive potential signals a reimagined ecosystem where technology serves as an enabler of equity, unlocking avenues for wealth creation that are adaptable and accessible.

AI's capacity to enhance decision-making also shines in its ability to identify trends and risks that relate not only to markets but also to personal financial health. Machine learning models excel at monitoring indicators that signal economic shifts, inflationary pressures, geopolitical developments, or sector rotations, feeding these insights back into financial strategies with remarkable agility. This anticipatory approach equips investors to hedge against downturns or capitalize on emerging opportunities before they become mainstream knowledge. On a personal level, AI's continuous analysis can detect signs of financial stress or vulnerability within a household budget—such as recurring overdrafts or escalating debt ratios—prompting timely interventions like debt restructuring advice or saving recommendations. The integration of AI-driven financial wellness platforms thus deepens the relationship between technology and holistic financial stewardship. By bridging macroeconomic intelligence with micro-level execution, AI ensures that decision-making is both responsive and strategic, underpinning a comprehensive framework for sustainable wealth growth.

Another dimension of AI's impact is its ability to foster interdisciplinary collaboration between human judgment and machine precision. While AI can process and analyze data at extraordinary scales, it thrives best when paired with human values, goals, and contextual awareness. The synergy between AI and human advisors generates enriched perspectives where emotionally nuanced decision-making meets algorithmic insight. This partnership is particularly salient in complex financial scenarios involving estate planning, philanthropy, or impact investing, where AI can model outcomes, but human discretion ensures alignment with personal ethics and legacy aspirations. Similarly, entrepreneurs utilizing AI-driven market intelligence can make better strategic pivots and resource allocations that reflect both quantitative analysis and human creativity. This interplay magnifies overall decision quality, reinforcing the theme that wealth creation is a human-centered endeavor empowered by technology rather than replaced by it. The optimal use of AI in financial decision-making, therefore, recognizes machines as indispensable collaborators, accelerating knowledge, expanding possibilities, and reducing friction—while humans remain the architects of vision and values.

Looking toward the future, AI's role in financial decision-making promises continued evolution with the integration of emerging technologies such as blockchain, quantum computing, and augmented reality. These advancements will further refine data security, transaction speed, and experiential interfaces, creating even more immersive and trustworthy environments for financial management. For instance, quantum computing's potential to solve complex optimization problems could revolutionize portfolio construction and risk assessment, revealing investment opportunities that current algorithms cannot detect. Augmented reality may transform how consumers interact with budgeting tools or financial markets by overlaying real-time data within intuitive visual contexts, enriching understanding and engagement. AI-driven predictive analytics might also evolve toward greater explainability and transparency, addressing ethical concerns and fostering trust. These technological frontiers, paired with responsible innovation, hold promises for democratizing wealth-building capabilities on an unprecedented scale. As AI continues to mature, its integration into financial ecosystems will become ever more seamless and personalized, ultimately embedding smarter decision-making into the fabric of everyday life.

In practical terms, harnessing AI tools effectively requires individuals to cultivate digital literacy and adopt a mindset open to continuous learning and experimentation. Understanding the functionalities, strengths, and limitations of AI-enabled financial platforms empowers users to discern meaningful insights and avoid potential pitfalls such as algorithmic bias or data privacy vulnerabilities. The rapidly changing technological landscape necessitates vigilance in selecting credible tools, integrating AI insights with holistic financial planning, and maintaining active oversight to complement automated processes. Moreover, aligning AI usage with personal financial goals and ethical considerations ensures that technology serves as a vehicle for authentic empowerment rather than a source of dependency or speculative risk. Developing these competencies fosters resilience against disruption, enabling individuals to adapt to new AI capabilities and opportunities as they arise. In essence, successful financial decision-making powered by AI is as much about cultivating human judgment and intention as it is about leveraging sophisticated algorithms.

Ultimately, the integration of AI into financial decision-making marks a pivotal evolution in how wealth can be understood, managed, and multiplied. By automating routine tasks, enhancing analytical depth, unveiling hidden opportunities, and reinforcing discipline, AI transforms the journey toward financial freedom from a fragmented, reactive enterprise into a strategic, data-driven voyage supported by agile technologies. Its capacity to customize and personalize financial experiences shifts control back to the individual, fostering confidence and clarity in navigating complex economic realities. At the same time, the collaboration between human insight and AI precision elevates ethical stewardship and purpose-driven wealth creation, ensuring that financial success aligns with broader life values. As AI continues to unfold its promise, those who embrace its capabilities with wisdom and deliberate intention will unlock unprecedented potential for building lasting financial security and legacy. Thus, the fusion of artificial intelligence with financial decision-making is not simply a technological innovation—it is a profound catalyst for empowerment, opening new horizons for every aspirant striving to live a life of financial freedom defined by skill, strategy, and smart decisions.

Chapter 22: Automation and Efficiency

"Productivity is never an accident. It is always the result of commitment to excellence." — Paul J. Meyer

Key Takeaways

- Automation saves time and reduces costs.
- Systems improve consistency.
- Technology enhances financial management.
- Focus on high-value activities.
- Productivity increases profitability.
- Smart automation creates competitive advantage.
- Efficiency accelerates wealth creation.

In the rapidly evolving landscape of wealth creation, the pursuit of automation and efficiency through technology is not merely an advantage; it has become a fundamental necessity. The integration of artificial intelligence and emerging technologies into our daily workflows serves as a transformative engine, amplifying productivity, reducing operational costs, and unlocking new realms of opportunity that were previously unfathomable. To truly appreciate how these technological advances empower financial freedom, one must first understand the profound shift in how decisions are made and tasks are performed in an increasingly automated world.

At its core, artificial intelligence brings the unparalleled ability to process vast volumes of data with remarkable speed and accuracy. This capacity revolutionizes decision-making by allowing individuals and businesses to access insights not by intuition alone, but by analyzing complex patterns and trends within seemingly disparate data points. Traditional decision-making often falls prey to cognitive biases, limited information, or emotional influences, which can obscure the path toward optimal choices. By contrast, AI-powered tools employ algorithms that sift through an ocean of variables, tease out subtle correlations, and distill actionable intelligence designed to enhance financial strategies. This shift from guesswork to data-driven decision-making elevates one's potential to identify lucrative investment opportunities, optimize resource allocation, and anticipate market fluctuations before they ripple through the economy.

Beyond decision-making, automation fundamentally alters the texture of task execution by unburdening individuals from repetitive, time-consuming activities that add little strategic value. Routine processes such as data entry, transaction reconciliation, inventory management, and financial reporting can be seamlessly delegated to intelligent systems. These systems not only perform tasks with heightened accuracy but also operate continuously, unhindered by fatigue or error. The resultant liberation of human effort allows for a redirection of focus toward higher-order functions—creative problem-solving, strategic planning, relationship building, and leadership development—that drive the kind of innovation and value creation essential for substantial wealth accumulation. Moreover, eliminating mundane tasks through automation reduces overhead costs, enhances operational efficiency, and streamlines workflows, enabling both individuals and enterprises to scale their financial ambitions without a proportional increase in complexity or expense.

Emerging technologies extend the boundaries of what was once considered possible in trend identification and opportunity recognition. Machine learning models, for example, can detect subtle shifts in consumer behavior, emerging market dynamics, or nascent technological disruptions well before they become mainstream. For entrepreneurs and investors alike, this foresight is invaluable, offering a competitive edge in launching products, entering markets, or adjusting portfolios in rhythm with evolving conditions rather than lagging them. Such proactive engagement with data-driven foresight transforms uncertainty into strategic clarity, fostering resilience in volatile environments and amplifying the capacity for sustained growth.

With the convergence of automation and artificial intelligence, the wealth-building process ascends to a dynamic interplay of continuous feedback and adaptive learning. Intelligent systems not only execute programmed tasks but improve autonomously by learning from past outcomes, refining their algorithms, and suggesting new efficiencies. This iterative evolution resembles a form of digital intuition, continuously enhancing the quality and speed of work. For the modern wealth builder, embracing this self-optimizing mechanism translates to maintaining relevance and advantage in fast-moving economic ecosystems. Furthermore, as these technologies permeate various industries, they catalyze the creation of entirely new business models and revenue streams—ranging from personalized financial advisory services leveraging AI-based predictive analytics to automated trading platforms that operate round-the-clock across global markets. The rise of such innovations democratizes access to sophisticated tools once reserved for elite institutional players, thereby expanding the horizon of wealth-building possibilities for individuals at every income level.

Yet, it is critical to recognize that harnessing automation and efficiency is not a mere technological upgrade but a profound mindset shift. The challenge lies in integrating these tools thoughtfully and ethically into one's financial journey, cognizant of their limitations and potential pitfalls. Technology, despite its power, is not infallible; it requires human oversight, judgment, and continuous learning to prevent over-reliance on algorithms that might amplify errors or obscure nuanced realities. Developing a disciplined approach toward technology adoption—embracing its benefits while maintaining critical scrutiny—ensures that automation serves as an empowering ally rather than a passive crutch. This balance enhances not only short-term productivity and cost savings but also cultivates long-term sustainability grounded in deliberate, values-centered wealth creation.

In practical terms, the journey toward automation and efficiency begins with a clear evaluation of one's existing workflows and financial processes to identify bottlenecks, redundancies, and areas ripe for technological intervention. Whether it involves deploying AI-driven budgeting apps that track and categorize expenses in real-time or implementing customer relationship management systems that automate outreach and follow-ups, every incremental gain in efficiency liberates time and cognitive resources essential for strategic growth. Entrepreneurs might leverage intelligent inventory systems that dynamically adjust stock levels, minimizing carrying costs while ensuring readiness to meet demand. Investors could utilize algorithmic trading bots calibrated to specific risk tolerances, thereby automating routine portfolio adjustments while freeing mental bandwidth for broader market analysis and strategic thinking. These examples illustrate that automation is not a one-size-fits-all solution; it demands customization aligned with unique goals, risk profiles, and operational realities.

Furthermore, the integration of emerging technologies is intrinsically tied to building a robust ecosystem of complementary tools and human skills. For automation to truly deliver on its promise of efficiency, individuals and organizations must invest in digital literacy, cultivating the capacity to interpret AI insights critically and adapt workflows accordingly. This dual capability—harnessing machine speed and human judgment—is what unlocks the full potential of automation in wealth creation. Consider the role of natural language processing in analyzing unstructured data such as news articles, social media trends, or industry reports, which can inform real-time investment decisions or entrepreneurial pivots. While AI algorithms can rapidly process this information, human interpretation is vital to contextualize findings within broader economic and sociopolitical frameworks, ensuring that decisions are not made in a vacuum but are deliberately connected to overarching strategic objectives.

The ripple effects of automation extend beyond individual efficiency gains, fostering collaborative synergy that multiplies wealth-building potential. By automating routine communication and coordination tasks, teams can focus on innovation, market expansion, and relationship cultivation, the human elements that technology cannot replicate. This symbiotic relationship between technology and human effort galvanizes collective productivity, reduces friction in complex operations, and creates scalable pathways for growth. Across industries, we witness how AI-powered platforms facilitate peer-to-peer lending, automated financial advising, and real-time market analysis, democratizing access to financial instruments and investment opportunities. This democratization levels the playing field, enabling more aspiring wealth builders to participate meaningfully in wealth accumulation beyond traditional gatekeeper models.

Moreover, the relentless march of technological progress continuously refines automation capabilities, embedding them ever deeper into the fabric of economic life. Edge computing, quantum algorithms, and blockchain integration promise to usher in new waves of efficiency and security, expanding the toolkit available to those committed to intelligent wealth building. Blockchain's capacity to provide transparent, tamper-proof transaction records reduces trust barriers and transaction costs, revolutionizing not only currency exchange but also asset management, contract execution, and identity verification. When combined with AI-driven automation, these technologies create environments where financial processes become seamless, secure, instantaneous, and decentralized, empowering individuals with unprecedented control over their financial destinies.

At the same time, ethical considerations must guide the deployment of automation and AI in wealth creation. Issues such as data privacy, algorithmic bias, and the social impact of workforce automation merit careful attention to ensure that technological progress contributes to equitable and responsible prosperity. For the aspiring wealth builders, embracing technology must be accompanied by a commitment to ethical principles that preserve human dignity, promote inclusivity, and foster sustainable economic ecosystems. This ethical anchor prevents the pursuit of efficiency from devolving into exploitation or short-sighted gain, aligning the quest for wealth not only with personal goals but with broader societal well-being.

Ultimately, the story of automation and efficiency in wealth building is one of empowerment—where technology serves as an enabling force that magnifies human potential without replacing it. In mastering the art of integration, wealth creators unlock the ability to work smarter rather than harder, optimize resources with precision, and navigate complexity with confidence. The path forward is one of continuous evolution, where the fusion of intelligent machines and discerning minds drives relentless progress toward financial freedom. By embracing automation and efficiency with both enthusiasm and caution, readers can position themselves at the vanguard of this transformative era, crafting not only wealth but a legacy defined by innovation, resilience, and purpose-driven success.

Chapter 23: Emerging Opportunities in Tech

"The future belongs to those who prepare for it today." — Malcolm X

Key Takeaways

- Technology creates new markets.
- Digital transformation rewards innovators.
- Stay informed about emerging trends.
- Develop future-ready skills.
- Adaptability fuels long-term success.
- Innovation creates wealth opportunities.
- Lifelong learning is essential in the digital economy.

The continuous surge of technological advancements is reshaping the very foundation of how wealth is generated, managed, and expanded in our contemporary world. Emerging technologies, particularly artificial intelligence (AI), blockchain, machine learning, biotechnology, and the Internet of Things (IoT), are not merely tools of convenience but powerful catalysts opening unprecedented avenues for creating and multiplying wealth. To recognize and capitalize on these new frontiers requires more than awareness; it demands an adaptive mindset, a readiness to learn, and the agility to pivot strategies swiftly with the evolving technological landscape. One of the most profound impacts of these technologies lies in their ability to revolutionize decision-making processes that were once constrained by human limitations and cognitive biases. AI algorithms can now analyze oceans of data in seconds, extracting relevant patterns and insights that might take human experts weeks or months to uncover. This accelerated data processing enables businesses and individuals alike to make smarter, faster, and more informed financial decisions, reducing risks and optimizing outcomes in real time. It's a remarkable shift from intuition-based choices to evidence-based strategies, allowing wealth builders to anticipate market shifts, consumer behavior, and emerging trends with remarkable precision.

Automation complements this shift by freeing up valuable human resources from repetitive, mundane tasks, enabling focus on strategic thinking, creativity, and leadership, the qualities that technology cannot easily replicate. The vast growth of robotic process automation (RPA) and AI-powered assistants now handles activities ranging from customer service to complex financial reconciliations, drastically improving operational efficiency and reducing costs. This liberation of time creates an explosion of opportunities for entrepreneurs and professionals to innovate, explore new ventures, and build human capital, the core asset for sustainable wealth creation. More importantly, this transformation is not confined to large corporations or tech giants; it trickles down to individuals, small businesses, and startups who harness accessible tools such as cloud computing, AI-driven analytics platforms, and automated marketing solutions to compete on a global stage. The democratization of technology effectively levels the playing field and opens wealth-building pathways once reserved for the elite, facilitating an ecosystem where nimble, tech-savvy players can disrupt industries and carve niches.

Beyond enhancing efficiency and decision-making, emerging technologies act as powerful engines of innovation, spawning wholly new industries and redefining traditional markets. Blockchain technology, with its decentralized and transparent ledger system, has given rise to cryptocurrencies and decentralized finance (DeFi), creating alternative means of investment, lending, and wealth accumulation that bypass conventional banking institutions. Early adopters have witnessed significant financial gains as new assets and protocols emerge, reshaping how wealth exchange is conceptualized. Similarly, the rise of the gig economy, empowered by digital platforms and ride-sharing applications, has democratized income generation and flexible work models, blending technology with human initiative to expand personal financial horizons. The expanding field of biotechnology and health tech offers another fertile ground, particularly as AI accelerates drug discovery, personalized medicine, and health data analytics, generating business opportunities for innovators who turn scientific breakthroughs into profitable ventures.

Furthermore, the aggregation and interpretation of real-time data generated by IoT devices offer enormous potential for industries ranging from agriculture to manufacturing. Smart sensors can optimize supply chains, reduce waste, and improve product quality, boosting profitability. This technology also paves the way for new business models centered around data subscription services, predictive maintenance, and customized consumer experiences, all of which open fresh routes to revenue generation. For wealth builders, the ability to understand and leverage these technological currents is akin to possessing a compass in an ever-shifting terrain—those who embrace these evolutions early gain competitive advantages elusive to slower adopters. Financial markets themselves are becoming more intertwined with algorithmic trading powered by sophisticated AI models that can predict price movements, hedge risks, and identify arbitrage opportunities with remarkable accuracy. Such capabilities create complex yet rewarding environments for investors who combine traditional insight with technological prowess, blending the art and science of wealth management.

Nonetheless, diving into these emerging opportunities requires not only enthusiasm but also critical discernment and ethical consideration. The rapid pace of innovation can outstrip existing regulatory frameworks, leading to ambiguities and risks, including cybersecurity threats, privacy concerns, and potential market volatility. Investing in speculative technologies demands rigorous due diligence and a deep understanding of both technical intricacies and market dynamics. This dimension of technology use invites wealth creators to cultivate a holistic approach that balances boldness with prudence and innovation with responsibility. Personal education and professional development in technology become non-negotiable assets, equipping individuals to navigate disruptions skillfully. In addition, seeking collaborative relationships with experts across disciplines—technologists, data scientists, legal advisors—can amplify the capacity to harness technology effectively and ethically. This integrative approach enriches decision-making frameworks and aligns wealth-building efforts with long-term sustainability and social impact.

At its core, the wealth opportunities emerging from technology are deeply intertwined with human creativity, leadership, and strategic foresight. Technologies provide horsepower, but it is human ingenuity that steers toward meaningful value creation. Entrepreneurs who identify unmet needs and design solutions leveraging AI and related technologies unlock vast markets and create transformative products and services that redefine industries. For established enterprises, adopting advanced technologies revitalizes their competitive edge, enabling them to innovate faster, customize offerings, and deliver superior customer experiences. On a personal level, developing technological competencies enhances employability, career progression, and the ability to participate actively as investors, consumers, and creators within the digital economy. This paradigm shift calls for lifelong learning as a foundational discipline, where understanding coding basics, data analytics, and AI tools becomes part of the core skillset for anyone serious about wealth building in the 21st century.

Moreover, the integration of AI and emerging technologies fuels what might be described as a wealth acceleration cycle—a virtuous loop where technology-driven insights lead to smarter investments, which generate financial returns that are then reinvested into further technological adoption and innovation. This compounding effect amplifies wealth potential exponentially when managed with clear objectives and strategic discipline. Examples abound of startups leveraging machine learning models to optimize marketing spend and improve conversion rates, enabling rapid scaling with minimal overhead. Similarly, fintech firms have revolutionized access to capital through peer-to-peer lending and robo-advisory platforms, making wealth growth more accessible and personalized. These innovations signal the dawn of a new era where wealth is not merely accumulated passively but actively engineered with precision tools and intelligent systems supporting every decision.

In exploring new wealth avenues born from technology, it is also essential to consider the global and societal implications, as technological diffusion varies widely across regions and demographics. While connected urban centers reap early benefits, digital divides persist, raising questions about inclusive wealth creation and economic equity. Nevertheless, emerging technologies offer promise for leapfrogging traditional development models, creating opportunities in underserved markets through mobile banking, telemedicine, and virtual education platforms. Visionary wealth builders can tap into these frontier markets, combining technology-driven solutions with localized knowledge to meet unmet needs profitably and responsibly. This global perspective reinforces the theme that wealth creation through technology is not a zero-sum game but a dynamic process capable of generating value that uplifts communities as well as individuals.

Ultimately, the new frontiers of wealth in technology require embracing complexity, uncertainty, and rapid change as integral characteristics of the contemporary financial landscape. Success lies in cultivating a mindset that is both curious and cautious, innovative and disciplined, visionary and practical. Wealth accumulation through emerging tech is not the story of sudden windfalls but of patient, informed engagement with evolving tools and trends. It involves building ecosystems of learning, experimentation, and adaptation, where skills and technology complement each other symbiotically. This approach transforms wealth from a solitary pursuit into a collaborative and continuous journey reflecting broader personal and societal aspirations. The immense possibilities unlocked by AI and other emerging technologies herald a landscape where the boundaries between creator and consumer, investor and innovator, learner and leader blur—ushering in a new paradigm of financial freedom intelligently designed for those ready to meet its challenges and seize its promises with wisdom and intentionality.

Chapter 24:
Discipline and Habits for Wealth

"We are what we repeatedly do. Excellence, then, is not an act but a habit." — Will Durant (summarizing Aristotle)

Key Takeaways

- Financial success depends on consistent habits.
- Discipline outperforms motivation.
- Daily choices shape long-term results.
- Delayed gratification builds wealth.
- Small improvements compound over time.
- Consistency creates extraordinary outcomes.
- Success is built through routine.

Goal Setting and Planning

Setting clear financial goals and building actionable plans around them is the cornerstone of any sustainable wealth-building journey. The power of goal setting lies not merely in scribbling ambitions on a piece of paper, but in the meticulous crafting of objectives so vivid, so compelling, that they command your attention daily, becoming a non-negotiable part of your existence.

Financial freedom is rarely a serendipitous event; rather, it is the product of disciplined intention anchored by specific, measurable, achievable, relevant, and time-bound objectives—often abbreviated as SMART goals. This framework, while widely known, demands nuanced understanding and adaptation to individual circumstances, turning abstract dreams into concrete milestones. When you design your financial goals with this level of precision, you effectively create a roadmap: a directional compass that guides every decision and action. Achieving wealth is neither a sprint nor a distant dash but an evolutionary process dotted with incremental victories, setbacks, and recalibrations—all aligned tightly with your overarching vision.

To cultivate this, developing a routine that champions goal clarity and holds you accountable is critical. It is easy to fall prey to the overwhelming magnitude of wealth ambitions—saving for retirement, investing wisely, starting a business, or achieving debt freedom—especially when distractions abound and initial progress feels slow. Here, the power of daily rituals cannot be overstated. Carving out dedicated moments each day to review, refine, and recommit to your financial plan transforms passive hopes into active pursuits. This could manifest as a morning reflection session where you assess your progress, adjust your budget, or consume focused financial education content. The act of daily engagement with your goals nurtures a mental environment where your plans are alive and breathing, impervious to the fluctuation of motivation. Discipline, in this context, is less about strict deprivation or punishment and more about consistent, small choices aligned with your highest priorities. It is the quiet, persistent force that keeps you tethered to your commitment, even on days when enthusiasm wanes.

Time management is naturally intertwined with goal setting and planning. Wealth building demands a judicious allocation of your most finite resource: time. How you choose to spend the hours and minutes in your day directly influences your capacity to accumulate assets, increase your skills, and expand your network. Effective time management, therefore, is not about cramming every minute with action but about prioritizing efforts that yield the highest leverage towards your financial objectives. This means distinguishing between tasks that are urgent versus important, understanding the difference between busywork and strategic moves, and proactively scheduling time blocks for deep focus activities such as research, investment analysis, or entrepreneurial pursuits. Advanced practitioners of goal planning often adopt techniques like time blocking, where the day is compartmentalized into pre-allocated segments dedicated solely to financial growth tasks, thus safeguarding these periods from distractions. The ability to say no—to invitations, projects, or habits that do not serve your goals—is a powerful manifestation of time mastery and an often-overlooked pillar of sustained wealth creation.

Mapping out a financial goal without a detailed plan is akin to setting sail without a chart. The plan is both compass and anchor—it charts the course and keeps you grounded when storms of uncertainty arise. Crafting an actionable plan involves more than listing what you want; it demands identifying the exact steps, resources, and timelines to bridge from here to there. For instance, if your objective is to save $50,000 over five years for an investment portfolio, your plan must specify monthly savings targets, spending adjustments, potential income enhancements, and contingencies for unforeseen expenses. Strategic foresight is crucial, requiring you to anticipate obstacles and build resilience into your roadmap. It is beneficial to break macro-goals into micro-goals, creating a hierarchy of achievements that provide regular feedback and motivation. Such granularity facilitates tracking and helps convert seemingly overwhelming ambitions into digestible, achievable chunks. Additionally, incorporating flexibility ensures your plan can evolve in response to life's unpredictability while maintaining fidelity to the core vision.

Beyond the technicalities of schedules and targets, self-discipline plays an equally significant role in sustaining momentum. In the realm of financial planning, self-discipline transcends mere willpower; it embodies a profound understanding that every choice—whether to spend on a fleeting desire or invest in long-term security—reflects a commitment to the life you ultimately want to lead. Establishing boundaries, developing patience, and fostering delayed gratification become daily practices embedded within your lifestyle. Self-discipline also involves cultivating emotional awareness to recognize when impulsive decisions or societal pressures threaten to derail your course. Successful wealth builders often employ techniques like accountability partnerships, journaling progress, or utilizing reminder systems that reinforce the discipline muscle. Equally important is celebrating milestones; acknowledging progress nourishes motivation and embeds positive reinforcement into the wealth-building routine. There is a transformational power in recognizing how small, consistent decisions accumulate over time, turning discipline from a daunting task into an empowering habit.

Integrating goal setting and planning with a growth mindset further amplifies your financial potential. A growth mindset—defined by openness to learning, resilience in the face of setbacks, and relentless curiosity—prepares you to adapt and innovate your strategies. This perspective transforms failures from final verdicts into invaluable lessons, recalibrating plans without abandoning foundational intentions. Within this framework, ongoing education isn't optional; it becomes a cornerstone habit. Seeking knowledge about market trends, financial instruments, tax regulations, and emerging technologies, especially in the digital finance spaces that your plans remain relevant and effective. The willingness to iterate and refine your goals in light of new information exemplifies strategic agility. For example, mastery of artificial intelligence tools can enhance your capacity to analyze investment opportunities or automate budgeting tasks, freeing up cognitive space for higher-level planning. Thus, your goal-setting practice remains dynamic, responsive, and future-ready, rather than static and brittle.

Relationships and community also weave profoundly into the fabric of effective goal setting and financial planning. Although the journey to wealth is deeply personal, involving other people creates opportunities and fortifies commitment. Engaging trusted mentors, coaches, or peer groups provides a vital sounding board and injects diverse perspectives into your strategy. These interactions offer motivation, wisdom gleaned from experience, and constructive feedback, all of which serve as accelerants to progress. Moreover, articulating your goals within a community creates social accountability, a subtle yet potent form of discipline supported by empathy and shared ambition. Collaborative endeavors, such as coinvesting or launching ventures with aligned partners, extend the reach of your plans beyond individual capacity, multiplying possibility through collective effort. The emotional support inherent in relationships also counteracts moments of doubt and isolation, common in protracted wealth-building processes. Thus, cultivating and leveraging networks is not ancillary but integral to planned financial success.

On a psychological level, crystallizing your "why" anchors your goal setting in deeper purpose rather than shallow desire. Wealth accumulation purely for status or consumption often lacks endurance; during inevitable challenges, such aims tend to lose their magnetic power. Conversely, a purpose-driven approach, whether rooted in family security, philanthropic impact, personal freedom, or creative expression, imbues your goals with meaning that sustains motivation even in adversity. Reflecting on your core values and long-term vision should precede detailed planning, ensuring alignment between financial objectives and identity. This alignment fosters coherence between what you do daily and who you aspire to be, integrating wealth-building seamlessly into your narrative rather than as an external pursuit. This unity of purpose and action generates energy that transcends mere habit, transforming the process into a profoundly fulfilling life journey. The famous adage that money is a tool, not the end, is fully realized here—wealth becomes an enabler of the life and legacy you envision.

As you chart your financial goals and construct plans to realize them, it is also imperative to build systems of measurement and reflection. Objective tracking enables course corrections and prevents them from drifting into complacency or reckless risk. Utilizing digital tools such as budgeting apps, investment trackers, or project management software can streamline this task, providing visual feedback on progress and flagging areas needing adjustment. Establishing regular reflection intervals—monthly or quarterly reviews, for example, allows for both tactical recalibration and strategic reassessment. This pauses the forward rush to ask critical questions: Are the goals still aligned with my values? Is my plan working as intended? What lessons have emerged? How can I optimize moving forward? Such structured introspection encourages proactive agility rather than reactive scrambling. It also enshrines a culture of accountability within your financial journey, creating momentum through clarity and transparency with yourself.

It is important to acknowledge that goal setting and planning are ongoing, iterative processes rather than singular events. Life's unpredictability—from economic cycles to personal development means that flexibility complements discipline. Wealth builders who learn to adapt goals and strategies in real time maintain resilience and avoid the trap of rigidity, which stifles growth. This balance is a nuanced art, requiring emotional intelligence to discern when to hold fast and when to pivot. Moreover, long-term planning benefits immensely from layering timescales: immediate objectives, medium-term ambitions, and visionary horizons. This tiered approach scaffolds complexity and nurtures both patience and urgency. It also allows the satisfaction of short-term wins while keeping an eye on transformative, multi-decade outcomes. Embedding such agility into your planning habits equips you not only for wealth accumulation but also for enduring prosperity amid shifting realities.

In the end, the practice of goal setting and planning for wealth transcends traditional boundaries of finance and becomes a lifestyle orientation. It intertwines intention with action, hope with rigor, ambition with humility. By establishing clear, meaningful financial objectives supported by structured routines, disciplined time management, and reflective practices, you build not only wealth but the capacity to sustain it indefinitely. This holistic approach elevates money from a transactional ledger to a dynamic narrative of growth, purpose, and freedom. Embarking on this path invites you into a lifelong partnership with your visionary, powerful journey where every step, however small, is a deliberate stride toward the life you were meant to live. The discipline to plan well and the courage to adapt are your greatest allies in unlocking this transformational potential, laying the foundation for a legacy that endures beyond material measures, rooted instead in wisdom, character, and the fulfillment of your highest aspirations.

Chapter 25: Time Management for Wealth

"The key is not spending time, but in investing it." — Stephen R. Covey

Key Takeaways

- Time is your most valuable asset.
- Prioritize activities that generate value.
- Eliminate distractions.
- Plan intentionally.
- Productivity supports financial growth.
- Invest time in learning and relationships.
- Every hour should move you toward your goals.

Time is the currency that underpins all wealth-building efforts, more precious than the dollars we seek to accumulate. It is the constant backdrop against which all our financial decisions and endeavors unfold, yet it remains one of the most elusive resources to master. The paradox of time in wealth creation is that everyone begins with the same 24 hours daily, but how those hours are directed and prioritized determines the richness of a person's financial future. The secret to sustained financial freedom does not reside solely in the size of one's income or investment portfolio but deeply within the discipline of managing time effectively. Prioritizing activities that maximize financial returns require more than just a to-do list or calendar hacks; it demands a holistic, intentional approach that integrates clear goal setting, rigorous self-discipline, strategic routine establishment, and mental fortitude to combat distractions and procrastination.

The essence of effective time management for wealth revolves around the principle of prioritization. This means that every action embarked on should be scrutinized through the lens of its potential to move the needle toward your financial objectives. It is not simply about being busy or productive in a general sense but focusing on activities that align directly with wealth-building outcomes. Too often, individuals fall into the trap of equating activity with progress, spending hours on tasks that yield little or no scalable financial benefit. For example, endless scrolling through social media or engagement in trivial errands might fill the day but do not contribute to human capital or financial capital growth. The disciplined investor or entrepreneur understands that time invested should generate compound returns, much like capital. Learning to say no to low-value tasks is as essential as saying yes to opportunities that stretch capacity and unlock new financial arenas.

Goal setting plays a foundational role in shaping effective time management, acting as a compass in the complex terrain of wealth creation. Without clear, measurable goals, time becomes a nebulous entity, prone to being wasted in inaction or misdirected effort. The practice of breaking down long-term financial aims into achievable short-term milestones infuses each day with purpose and direction. For instance, a goal of accumulating a certain net worth by retirement becomes more tangible when segmented into yearly savings targets, monthly investment reviews, or weekly skill-enhancement activities. Setting goals with a balanced combination of ambition and realism ensures motivation without overwhelming pressure, cultivating continuity rather than burnout. Furthermore, embedding these goals within a written framework or visual reminder strengthens commitment and eases the mental load of decision-making throughout the day. Reviewing and adjusting goals in response to changing circumstances is equally vital, as it keeps time management attuned to evolving realities and opportunities.

Building effective routines is the cornerstone of sustaining time management practices over a lifetime. Routines transform the chaotic flow of time into structured segments where focused work can occur. High achievers in financial domains often develop morning rituals that set the tone for the day—this might include reading market news, strategizing investments, or engaging in professional development exercises before the distractions of daily life take hold. The consistency of performing wealth-related tasks at designated times creates a rhythm that smooths productivity and reinforces discipline. Ritualized breaks and periods of reflection can be interwoven into routines to maintain mental sharpness and prevent fatigue, another key aspect of sustainable time management. Routines also serve as psychological anchors—when a person habitually dedicates their mornings to wealth-building activities, it cultivates a mindset of seriousness and intentionality that spreads into other life domains.

Self-discipline emerges as the weapon in the arsenal of time management, the force that protects the commitment to prioritization and routines against the ceaseless tides of distraction and temptation. It is the internal governance system that allows an individual to veto immediate gratification or easy options in favor of the long-term reward of financial freedom. Cultivating self-discipline involves practicing delayed gratification consistently, resisting the impulse to divert time towards less productive activities even when fatigue or stress presses. This is not merely an act of willpower but involves creating an environment conducive to focus—removing distractions, setting firm boundaries around work and leisure time, and training the mind to resist multitasking, which often fractures focus and wastes time. Additionally, self-discipline benefits immensely from accountability mechanisms: sharing goals with mentors, cohorts, or through digital tracking tools helps sustain motivation and provides external reinforcement in moments of wavering resolve.

A vital but often overlooked aspect of time management for wealth involves leveraging the concept of opportunity cost—the notion that time invested in one activity automatically precludes investment in another. This mental calculus encourages deliberate selection of tasks that yield the highest financial returns or build critical wealth-building skills. For example, attending networking events or professional development workshops is often more valuable than passive leisure activities because the relationships and knowledge gained can translate into future income streams or partnership opportunities. By contrast, spending excessive time on routine administrative tasks without delegation or automation can drain valuable hours better spent on high-impact work. Financially successful individuals often become adept at outsourcing or streamlining fewer essential functions, thus freeing their own time for activities that compound human capital or accelerate wealth growth.

Technology plays a growing and transformative role in contemporary time management strategies for wealth creation. Modern tools—from calendar applications integrated with artificial intelligence to project management platforms—offer capabilities that extend beyond simple scheduling to actual strategic prioritization and predictive analytics. These technologies can analyze workloads, suggest optimal task sequences, and highlight potential inefficiencies, thereby enabling higher precision in daily time allocation. Furthermore, digital time-management tools provide the ability to track how hours are spent with granular detail, uncovering hidden pockets of wasted time that, once reclaimed, can be redirected to income-generating or skill-building pursuits. Mastering the use of such technologies requires a proactive learning attitude and willingness to adapt processes to improve digital ecosystems, but the payoff is considerable in elevating daily productivity and preserving precious hours.

Integral to successful time management in financial contexts is understanding energy management, which is intimately linked to productivity cycles. Human beings operate in natural rhythms of high and low mental and physical energy; recognizing and adapting to these fluctuations enables optimal scheduling of demanding wealth-building activities. For instance, tasks requiring creative problem-solving or strategic thinking merit alignment with peak cognitive periods, typically early in the day for many individuals. Conversely, routine or administrative chores fit better into lower-energy slots to minimize resistance and exhaustion. Ignoring these rhythms not only diminishes efficiency but risks burnout and reduces motivation. Wealth creation is a marathon, not a sprint. Aligning time management with energy flow fosters sustainability and enhances overall output quality, reinforcing the discipline necessary to maintain consistent progress.

The psychological dimension of time management is equally critical. How one perceives time—whether as a threat, a scarce resource, or an abundant opportunity—shapes behaviors profoundly. A mindset anchored in scarcity, where time is viewed as perpetually insufficient, often leads to stress, indecision, and counterproductive multitasking. In contrast, adopting a growth-oriented time mindset, embracing time as a managed resource that can be optimized through learning and discipline, creates a foundation for calm, focused action. This shift from urgency to intentionality lays the groundwork for deep work, the kind of profound, uninterrupted concentration that research shows produces the highest value output. Embracing this mindset also improves resilience, allowing one to bounce back effectively from setbacks or interruptions without losing the thread of long-term financial plans.

It is also important to acknowledge that time management for wealth is not an isolated endeavor but intricately connected to the broader framework of life balance and well-being. Excessive fixation on financial pursuits at the expense of health, family, or personal fulfillment ultimately undermines the very freedom one seeks to establish. Wise individuals recognize that time devoted to rest, relationships, and rejuvenation is an investment that replenishes the mental clarity and emotional strength critical for effective wealth accumulation. This holistic appreciation compels the integration of non-financial priorities into daily planning, ensuring that time management serves a larger purpose beyond mere monetary gain. Achieving this balance requires conscious reflection and adjustment, tailoring routines and priorities to evolving life stages and values while keeping the financial vision intact.

Finally, time management in the context of building lasting wealth demands embracing continuous learning as a non-negotiable habit. The financial world and career landscapes evolve rapidly; staying abreast of new skills, market trends, and innovations, including technologies like artificial intelligence, require deliberate allocation of learning time. This might take the form of scheduled reading, courses, or engaging with expert communities. When the pursuit of knowledge becomes a routine embedded in the daily or weekly rhythm, it compounds over time, producing exponential improvements in decision-making and opportunities. The commitment to lifelong learning maximizes the efficiency of every minute invested, effectively unlocking new pathways to wealth previously inaccessible to the unprepared.

In sum, time management for wealth is not merely a tactical endeavor but a foundational discipline that shapes the entire trajectory of financial freedom. It requires a clear vision anchored in realistic goals, the establishment of empowering routines, the cultivation of unwavering self-discipline, and the ruthless prioritization of high-value tasks. This framework must be continuously refined with the aid of technological tools, while harmonizing with human energy cycles and psychological perspectives that favor intention over urgency. Moreover, it flourishes best when woven into a balanced life and fueled by committed learning. Those who master this intricate equation find that time, once the foe of financial freedom, becomes the greatest accelerant in their wealth-building journey, allowing them not only to accumulate resources but to live richly and purposefully every single day.

Chapter 26:
Consistency and Self-Discipline

"Successful people do consistently what unsuccessful people do occasionally." — Craig Groeschel

Key Takeaways

- Consistency creates lasting success.
- Self-discipline strengthens financial resilience.
- Small actions produce significant long-term results.
- Build routines that support your goals.
- Stay committed during difficult seasons.
- Persistence separates achievers from dreamers.
- Success is earned through daily discipline.

Consistency and self-discipline form the backbone of any meaningful journey toward financial freedom and lasting wealth. In the world of wealth creation, the sharpest strategies, the most brilliant business ideas, and the most advanced technologies will all falter without the steady hands of routine, unwavering commitment, and the ability to resist short-term temptations in favor of long-term rewards. The magic lies not in sporadic bursts of effort but in the sustained, measured progress that compounds over time—a process sustained and made possible only by cultivating habits that anchor growth, build resilience, and nurture a mindset tuned to perseverance. When we speak of consistency, we are referring to the day-in, day-out actions, decisions, and behaviors that seem small individually but collectively form the foundations upon which empires are built and lives transformed. Meanwhile, self-discipline is the inner strength that keeps us aligned with our greater purposes when distractions or discouragements threaten to pull us off track. Without these twin pillars, wealth-building efforts often become fleeting and fragile, vulnerable to the unpredictable currents of motivation, circumstance, and distraction.

Fundamentally, healthy consistency begins with the establishment of intentional routines—daily rhythms that align our time with our priorities. Life's chaos is one of the largest obstacles that erodes financial discipline; without deliberate structure, days slip away, leaving behind a trail of unmet goals and regrets. Crafting meaningful routines requires intentionality; it demands a thoughtful prioritization of what activities genuinely propel us toward our financial aspirations, stripping away the unnecessary clutter of non-essential tasks and time-wasters. This process of refining daily habits is not merely about productivity for its own sake but about building a sustainable ecosystem wherein positive actions become automatic, embedded in the fabric of daily life. Waking up each morning with a clear set of priorities or a modest plan—whether it be reviewing personal budgets, investing time in skill development, or networking—feeds into the momentum that sustained wealth generation demands. The greatest minds in business and finance, from Warren Buffett to Oprah Winfrey, share a common attribute: a powerful daily regimen that preserves focus despite the tide of distractions around them. They have honed their rituals to advance critical imperatives, transforming intention into habit.

Time management is an inseparable companion of consistency and self-discipline, and understanding its nuances is vital to sustaining growth over the long haul. Time is our most finite and precious resource, yet ironically, it is also the most neglected asset in wealth creation. Many squander it on trivial pursuits because they fail to recognize that every minute not harnessed intentionally is a step away from progress. Mastery of time management involves more than filling a schedule with activities; it requires learning to invest chunks of time on high-leverage tasks that yield outsized rewards. This often means resisting the siren call of immediacy, the email that must be answered now, the social media scroll, the endless distractions that fragment attention and deplete energy. Establishing blocks of uninterrupted time dedicated to focused work, commonly termed as deep work, nurtures productivity and the acquisition of valuable skills. Identifying peak energy periods in the day and aligning demanding tasks accordingly is another smart tactic to maximize output. Crucially, managing time well also involves carving out periods for rest and reflection. Burnout is a silent wealth killer, and without moments of recovery, consistency degrades into exhaustion and inconsistency. The interplay between focused effort and renewal forms a rhythm that sustains performance and mental clarity over the long journey of financial growth.

Goal setting is a critical compass that guides consistent action and fortifies self-discipline. Goals transform vague desires into concrete destinations, creating measurable benchmarks that can be tracked and celebrated. Yet not all goals wield the same power or effectiveness. Well-crafted goals are specific, measurable, achievable, relevant, and time-bound—principles famously encapsulated by the acronym SMART. This framework steers us away from nebulous wishes such as "I want to be rich" toward concrete aims like "I will save $10,000 for an emergency fund within 12 months." Setting smaller milestone goals provides manageable steps that weave a tapestry of progress, preventing overwhelm and offering continual motivation. Each milestone met builds confidence and reinforced discipline through positive feedback loops. Moreover, reframing setbacks and failures as learning opportunities rather than insurmountable defeats enables resilience, another key to long-term consistency. It is important to recognize that goals should not be static; revisiting and revising them as circumstances evolve keeps efforts purposeful and relevant. Aligning goals with internal values ensures they are not merely external measures of success but meaningful markers of personal fulfillment, which fuels sustained commitment.

Self-discipline, the ability to persist in actions that serve our long-term interests despite short-term impulses, often stands as the greatest hurdle and simultaneously the most transformative skill in wealth building. Discipline can be understood as a muscle that strengthens with regular exercise but weakens without use. Building self-discipline begins with developing awareness of one's own behavioral patterns and triggers—those moments of weakness or distraction when it becomes tempting to deviate from the planned course. Mindfulness practices, such as journaling emotions or reflecting on decisions, can deepen this understanding. Once aware, individuals can design their environments to minimize exposure to temptations; for example, automating savings contributions removes reliance on willpower for money management. Small, incremental acts of discipline—like resisting the impulse to make impulsive purchases, dedicating focused time each day to skill enhancement, or maintaining consistency in sleep schedules—create a reservoir of mental strength that supports more substantial challenges over time. Cultivating patience is also essential, as self-discipline prevents us from chasing immediate gratification in favor of delayed rewards that often prove far more substantial. Reinforcing discipline through accountability systems, such as check-ins with mentors, trusted peers, or even digital tracking tools, provides external support for internal commitment.

It's important to acknowledge that the path of consistency and discipline is not one of harsh austerity or rigid perfection but of balanced flexibility and compassionate persistence. Life inevitably presents unforeseen events, health challenges, family obligations, market downturns—that can disrupt even the best-laid plans. The key lies in developing resilience: the capacity to bounce back, recalibrate quickly, and continue moving forward despite setbacks. Building resilience often requires cultivating a growth mindset—the belief that abilities can be developed through effort and learning rather than being fixed traits. This mindset transforms obstacles into steppingstones; setbacks become feedback rather than failure. A resilient individual views consistency not as an unattainable standard of flawlessness but as a commitment to progression, however incremental. This perspective fuels emotional sustainability and guards against burnout, frustration, and discouragement. Indeed, self-discipline paired with self-compassion—the grace to forgive oneself yet recommit—creates a sustainable cycle in which the pursuit of wealth becomes a journey of evolving mastery rather than a punishing regime.

In practical terms, integrating consistency and self-discipline into the wealth-building process can take many forms tailored to individual circumstances and preferences. Some find success beginning their mornings with rituals that prepare their minds for productivity, such as meditation, journaling, or reviewing priorities, creating psychological readiness. Others leverage technology for habit tracking, calendaring, and reminders that reinforce intentional actions. For those who struggle with motivation, visualizing long-term goals through vision boards or narratives can heighten commitment by keeping the bigger picture vivid and emotionally charged. Creating a network of supportive relationships also bolsters discipline by fostering environments where positive behaviors are encouraged and accountability is normal. Importantly, learning to say no—to distractions, to time drains, to non-essential engagements—is a profound exercise in self-discipline, one that protects the precious resource of focus. Over time, as the disciplined habits grow stronger, tasks that once demanded enormous effort become smoother, forming a virtuous feedback loop of increased confidence and capability.

Moreover, the consistency and self-discipline required for wealth-building extend beyond purely financial tasks; they embrace continuous learning and personal growth, which are essential to adapt in an ever-changing economic landscape. The compound effect of daily reading, training, networking, and self-reflection enriches human capital, equipping individuals to navigate complexity and seize emerging opportunities. Disregarding this broader scope often limits growth and resilience, as static knowledge and skills become obsolete quickly in a world driven by technological change and innovation. Yet, the discipline to sustain learning amidst competing demands is often what separates those who maintain upward financial trajectories from those who stagnate. It is a commitment to lifelong growth that embodies true wealth, one that cannot be bought or inherited but must be cultivated patiently and consistently.

In an age increasingly shaped by rapid technology and artificial intelligence, consistency and self-discipline acquire an added dimension of strategic importance. Technology offers unparalleled tools to streamline financial management, automate investments, and provide insightful data—but without disciplined use, these instruments can become sources of distraction or overwhelm. Developing consistent practices around technological adoption, such as regularly reviewing portfolio performance or updating skills in AI tools, ensures these advances become allies rather than liabilities. Self-discipline is also critical in maintaining cybersecurity vigilance, budgeting for digital subscriptions, and navigating the ever-expanding landscape of financial products thoughtfully. Harnessing technology with discipline magnifies the compounding effects of consistent effort, accelerating wealth creation while mitigating risks in a complex, interconnected world.

Finally, it is essential to recognize that the rewards of consistency and self-discipline transcend monetary wealth alone. They forge character and cultivate virtues such as patience, perseverance, humility, and integrity. These qualities not only elevate financial outcomes but enrich life itself, building reputations of reliability and trust that open doors to new opportunities and meaningful relationships. Wealth achieved without discipline often proves ephemeral, but wealth grounded in consistent habits and steadfast resolve builds a legacy, shaping not only financial futures but generational trajectories. The journey may demand grit and sacrifice, but it also yields profound fulfillment—a life marked not just by material abundance but by a deep sense of accomplishment and alignment with purpose. Hence, committing to consistency and self-discipline is the most profound investment one can make, the true "secret sauce" behind the wealth equation. It sets the stage for every other strategy, skill, and innovation to flourish, creating a sturdy, resilient foundation upon which dreams become reality.

Chapter 27:
Purpose-Driven Wealth Building

"Success without fulfillment is the ultimate failure."
— Tony Robbins

Key Takeaways

- Wealth should serve a meaningful purpose.
- Values should guide financial decisions.
- Financial success is more fulfilling when aligned with purpose.
- Legacy matters more than possessions.
- Stewardship creates lasting impact.
- Purpose inspires disciplined action.
- True wealth benefits others as well as yourself.

Aligning Wealth with Values

In the realm of wealth creation, the pursuit of financial prosperity often encounters a crossroads where the glitter of monetary gain must reconcile with the deeper currents of personal ethics and genuine passions. Wealth, when considered solely as a numerical accumulation or a transactional achievement, runs the risk of becoming an empty pursuit—one disconnected from the essence of who we are and what we ultimately seek to contribute to the world. It is here, in the deliberate act of aligning wealth with values, that a profound transformation occurs, shaping not only the trajectory of financial success but also the quality and meaning of that success. This alignment serves as a compass, guiding decisions, nurturing motivation, and ensuring that the fruits of one's labor are not merely transient tokens of material achievement, but seeds planted toward a legacy rich with purpose and integrity.

The foundation of this alignment is rooted deeply in understanding what truly matters to the individual beyond societal definitions of success. Personal ethics and core values act as an inner framework, a lodestar by which all financial endeavors are measured and refined. The journey begins with a reflective immersion into one's beliefs, passions, and moral compass—questions that often get overlooked in the haste of professional ambition or the allure of quick financial wins. By confronting these essential questions—What principles will I never compromise? What drives my spirit with genuine fervor? How do I wish to impact others and the broader society? Individuals cultivate clarity and intentionality in their wealth-building strategies. This clarity, in turn, becomes a powerful motivator, anchoring efforts through the inevitable challenges and complexities of the path to financial freedom.

Purpose and meaning become inseparable allies to discipline and strategy when wealth pursuits are infused with values. While the mechanics of investing, business acumen, or career advancement are critical, they become exponentially more influential when tethered to a sense of mission. This interdependence fuels resilience; a person anchored to a meaningful cause is less likely to succumb to discouragement or ethical shortcuts. Instead, their endeavors are animated by a continuing narrative that transcends the immediate gains. Wealth is reframed not as an end but as a vehicle resource that amplifies impact, nurtures relationships, and supports causes aligned with deeper convictions. Such a mindset shifts the paradigm from scarcity-driven accumulation to abundance-oriented stewardship, where resources are managed thoughtfully with an awareness of their potential to create positive ripple effects.

Ethical wealth creation is not simply idealistic rhetoric but a practical framework that fosters sustainable success. It challenges the pervasive notion that financial achievement necessitates compromise or exploitation, offering instead a model where honesty, fairness, and social responsibility are integral. In practice, this means making business and investment choices that honor the dignity of people and the planet. It involves scrutinizing opportunities through lenses of transparency, environmental stewardship, and social impact, thereby embedding a conscientious approach into the core of financial activity. Such an approach often opens doors to new avenues of growth; trustworthiness builds stronger networks, consumer loyalty deepens, and partnerships flourish. Over time, the alignment of wealth with values cultivates a reputation that is itself an asset, creating a virtuous cycle where ethical conduct enhances financial returns.

The dimension of passion bears a vital connection to this ethical and values-driven framework. Passion is the emotional energy that ignites innovation, endurance, and creativity. It is the flame that sustains motivation long after the initial excitement wanes, enabling individuals to navigate the complexities of building wealth with a sense of joy and purpose. When financial endeavors are congruent with what one truly loves, whether it is advancing social justice, nurturing communities, creating art, or contributing to technological progress, there is an intrinsic fuel that propels consistent effort and continuous learning. This passionate engagement transforms routine transactions and strategies into expressions of authentic identity, infusing the wealth-building process with meaning that money alone could never buy.

The impact of wealth aligned with values extends far beyond the individual's bank balance; it resonates within the legacy one leaves behind. Legacy in this context transcends the transmission of material assets; it is the enduring imprint of character, vision, and intentional action. When wealth is built and managed with a clear ethical framework and a passionate purpose, it becomes a catalyst for transformation that echoes across generations. This might manifest as support for educational initiatives that empower future leaders, investments that foster sustainable communities, or philanthropic endeavors that bridge disparities. Such a legacy shapes the narrative of a life well-lived narrative that inspires others to pursue wealth not for mere accumulation but to cultivate a world imbued with justice, opportunity, and compassion.

Moreover, the process of aligning wealth with values invites a redefinition of what it means to be truly wealthy. It encourages a holistic perspective that embraces not only financial capital but also social capital, intellectual capital, and spiritual fulfillment. Wealth, in this expanded view, is the harmonious integration of these dimensions, where money serves as a tool to facilitate enrichment in all areas of life. This redefinition challenges the relentless chase for more without regard to consequence, replacing it with a rhythm of mindful acquisition and purposeful distribution. Such mindfulness fosters a deep satisfaction that affirms a person's identity and contributions in a way that transient pleasures never could.

Embracing this alignment requires courage and continual self-awareness, as it often necessitates making difficult choices that may diverge from conventional paths or immediate gains. The temptation to prioritize short-term profits over long-term values can be strong, especially in competitive or uncertain environments. Yet, those who commit to this alignment often discover that their integrity becomes a fortress, providing clarity and confidence amid ambiguity. They learn to listen to their inner voice as they navigate financial decisions, cultivating an inner harmony that reflects in their external successes. This integrity builds bridges, drawing like-minded collaborators and forging relationships grounded in trust and mutual respect.

In addition, this approach to wealth building invites a dynamic interplay between personal growth and financial strategy. As individuals deepen their understanding of their values and passions, they often experience an expansion of perspective that influences their approach to money management and investment. Choices become more reflective, strategic not only for financial gain but also for alignment with broader life goals and societal contributions. This growth is continuous, requiring regular reflection and adjustment, mirroring the evolving nature of values as life unfolds. The journey of integrating wealth with values thus becomes a lifelong practice of refinement, where each success and setback offers lessons that shape a more coherent, meaningful financial narrative.

The influence of technology and artificial intelligence further amplifies the possibilities for aligning wealth creation with values. These tools provide unprecedented access to data, analytics, and platforms that can be harnessed to identify and engage in ethical investments, socially responsible businesses, and innovative ventures that resonate with personal missions. They enable transparency and accountability, allowing individuals to track the impact of their financial decisions closely and adjust accordingly. The intelligent use of these technologies facilitates a more informed and deliberate approach to wealth management, one that reinforces, rather than dilutes, the commitment to value-based success. In this way, progress in financial technology does not merely enhance efficiency but becomes a partner in realizing wealth that is conscious and congruent with one's deepest convictions.

Ultimately, ensuring that financial pursuits reflect personal ethics and passions transforms the concept of wealth into a living, breathing expression of identity and purpose. It transcends transactional thinking and embraces a holistic narrative where money is both a resource and a responsibility. This alignment cultivates a profound sense of fulfillment, as individuals witness their efforts contributing to causes and communities, they deem worthy. It inspires a deeper connection between their work and to others, fostering a sense of belonging and shared progress. By weaving values into the fabric of financial strategy, wealth creation becomes an enriching journey of self-discovery, impact, and legacy—one that invites each person to contribute uniquely to the tapestry of human advancement, not merely through profits but through principles and passion.

Chapter 28: Philanthropy and Giving Back

"No one has ever become poor by giving." — Anne Frank

Key Takeaways

- Generosity multiplies impact.
- Giving strengthens communities.
- Wealth creates opportunities to serve others.
- Philanthropy reflects responsible stewardship.
- Success carries social responsibility.
- Giving builds lasting fulfillment.
- A generous life creates an enduring legacy.

Philanthropy and giving back occupy a profoundly transformative role within the broader narrative of wealth creation, imbuing what might otherwise be a purely transactional or numerical pursuit with purpose, meaning, and enduring human dimension. Wealth that remains confined to bank accounts or material possessions risks becoming hollow, a testament to success measured merely by accumulation rather than impact. The purposeful act of sharing one's wealth—whether financial resources, time, expertise, or networks—rethinks wealth not just as an end, but as a way to cultivate growth, healing, and opportunity in the world beyond the self. It is within this dynamic process that philanthropy becomes a formidable pillar of sustainable wealth strategy, marrying the pragmatism of financial prowess with the ethical imperative to contribute, uplift, and build a legacy that transcends the individual lifetime. This deeper relationship between wealth and generosity reshapes motivation at its core. When financial ambition is tethered to values that emphasize giving, it elevates the pursuit of monetary success from mere survival or comfort to a journey anchored in meaning and communal advancement. The drive to build wealth, therefore, gains an enriching layer, one that widens the lens through which success is viewed—not just as personal fulfillment but as the capacity to make tangible differences in the lives of others.

At the heart of this transformative cycle lies the recognition that wealth affords agency—agency to address social inequities, to nurture education, to foster innovation that benefits humanity, and to fortify communities against cyclical hardships. When individuals or institutions integrate philanthropy into their financial ecosystems, they reimagine the role of money as a dynamic instrument of change, not a static endpoint. These reframing challenges conventional attitudes that sometimes equate giving with sacrifice or loss, revealing instead that generosity fuels both internal satisfaction and external impact, creating a virtuous cycle where abundant resources multiply through purposeful deployment. The act of giving back resounds well beyond the immediate benefit it confers; it shapes social narratives around wealth itself, shifting perceptions from accumulation for accumulation's sake to wealth as stewardship—an ethical responsibility to nurture what has been entrusted. This mindset nurtures character, discipline, and a sense of humility in the face of privilege, qualities that reinforce sustainable financial habits and thoughtful leadership. It is a reminder that true wealth is as much about what we contribute as it is about what we keep, and that the most enduring legacies are those etched in the lives we touch and the systems we help to uplift.

Philanthropy's contribution to motivation is nuanced and deeply psychological. Human beings are wired to seek purpose and meaning beyond material gain and giving back answers this existential yearning with profound resonance. When philanthropic efforts align with personal values and passions, they create a compelling "why" that sustains perseverance amid the inevitable challenges of building and managing wealth. This anchoring purpose transforms routine financial milestones into symbolic steps toward broader aspirations, cultivating resilience and a sustained sense of fulfillment. Moreover, the act of generosity cultivates emotional richness, enriching one's experience of wealth with joy, gratitude, and connectedness. This psychological dimension cannot be overstated; wealth devoid of such qualities can breed isolation, anxiety, and an insatiable desire for more, whereas generosity engenders a sense of belonging and transcendence. It is in these moments of giving, when the veil drops between self and other, that the potential for true wealth—to live abundantly and to help others do the same—becomes palpable.

From an ethical standpoint, incorporating philanthropy into wealth strategy counters the transactional tendencies that sometimes pervade capitalist frameworks. It reminds us that financial success is not solely a private endeavor insulated from societal responsibility, but rather a privileged position from which one can influence social structures. Ethical wealth creation embraces transparency, accountability, and the intentional use of resources to foster equitable progress. Philanthropy, far from being a peripheral luxury, becomes a vital expression of this ethic, ensuring that wealth creation does not perpetuate inequality or harm but instead promotes justice, inclusion, and empowerment. This ethical grounding provides a compass in navigating complex decisions around investments, business practices, and partnership opportunities, aligning economic goals with a moral vision. It challenges the paradigm that profitability must come at the expense of people or the planet, instead envisioning a model where wealth amplifies positive outcomes across multiple stakeholders.

The impact of philanthropy also extends to the concept of legacy, a theme inseparable from the deeper ambitions of wealth-building for many. Legacy, in this respect, crystallizes as the lasting imprint left by one's financial choices and actions on future generations. It transcends the mere inheritance of money, encompassing the transmission of values, vision, and the capacity to sustain good in perpetuity. Philanthropic activities embedded within a wealth strategy can architect this legacy through foundations, scholarships, community programs, or social enterprises; each designed to endure beyond the founder's lifespan and adapt to evolving needs. This legacy is nurtured not just by the size of the endowment or the visibility of grand gestures, but by the intentional cultivation of structures that empower others to thrive autonomously. Therefore, giving back as a strategic habit in one's journey is deeply interwoven with a narrative about timelessness—the aspiration to create ripples of positive change that extend, multiply, and diversify long after one's direct involvement ceases.

The social dimensions of philanthropy further illuminate how generosity acts as a conduit for building and strengthening relationships, networks, and communities—essential elements in wealth creation. When individuals engage authentically in giving, they often encounter a broader purpose that connects them to causes and people beyond their immediate circles. This expanded social capital, characterized by trust, shared goals, and mutual support, can open doors to collaborative ventures, partnerships, and innovative solutions that might otherwise remain inaccessible. Philanthropy thus enriches not only the beneficiaries but also the givers, who gain perspective, inspiration, and renewed energy to pursue their financial and personal goals. In this way, generosity becomes a strategic lever that interweaves human connection with fiscal growth, producing a holistic fabric of wealth that includes social and emotional dimensions.

Moreover, contemporary technology and data analytics have ushered in a renaissance in philanthropy that makes giving more strategic and impactful than ever before. The emerging field of effective altruism, for example, uses rigorous evaluation and evidence to direct resources where they will yield the greatest benefit, marrying compassion with discipline. Wealth creators who integrate such approaches within their giving strategies harness tools like artificial intelligence, big data, and precision metrics to assess the effectiveness of initiatives, optimize resource allocation, and track outcomes over time. This infusion of technology into philanthropy echoes the same demand for efficiency and accountability that characterizes successful business enterprises, thereby elevating giving from goodwill to a sophisticated, results-oriented practice. Incorporating these modern techniques into a broader wealth equation not only maximizes impact but also reinforces the principle that generosity is an integral, thoughtfully managed component of the financial ecosystem.

On a personal level, the practice of philanthropy invites individuals to cultivate humility and gratitude, qualities that are often undervalued in discussions of financial success. The recognition that wealth and opportunity are not solely the result of personal effort but often emerge from a confluence of privilege, timing, and support encourages a mindful perspective that contrasts sharply with entitlement or ego-driven pursuits. Giving back is a continual reminder of interconnectedness—that no one thrives in isolation and that redistributing surplus resources honors this fundamental truth. This humility, in turn, fosters deeper empathy and a lifelong commitment to learning and growth as one continually seeks to improve methods of contribution. It positions philanthropy as a dynamic practice, not merely a one-time act, aligning with the book's overarching theme of continuous growth and learning.

Educational philanthropy bears particular importance in this context, as investment in human capital often yields exponential returns for societies and economies alike. Supporting education, whether through scholarships, institutional endowments, or innovative learning initiatives, empowers others to develop critical skills, leadership capacities, and entrepreneurial mindsets essential for sustaining wealth creation over generations. This cyclical effect—where the fruits of one's success, enable the rise of others' potential—reinforces abundance of thinking, counteracting scarcity mentalities that undermine collaboration and progress. It embeds giving back within a forward-looking framework, where contributions serve not just immediate needs but also the cultivation of future change-makers capable of driving systemic transformation.

Entrepreneurial philanthropy, too, exemplifies how innovative approaches to giving can amplify systemic impact. Rather than traditional charity models that may address symptoms, entrepreneurial philanthropy deploys capital with an emphasis on sustainability, scalability, and measurable outcomes. Social enterprises funded by such philanthropy integrate business acumen with social missions, demonstrating that financial returns and social goods need not be mutually exclusive. For the wealth creator, investing in these hybrid ventures represents both a commitment to purpose and a strategic avenue to diversify financial portfolios while reinforcing values-driven decision-making. This model of philanthropy, therefore, aligns seamlessly with the book's call to integrate skills, strategy, and smart decisions in pursuit of a holistic wealth-building paradigm.

Philanthropy also exerts influence within the family wealth context, shaping intergenerational dynamics and legacy planning. Introducing the values of giving and stewardship early in family wealth education helps to cultivate responsible attitudes among heirs, mitigating risks of entitlement and disengagement. When families commit to shared philanthropic goals, they foster unity, collective purpose, and a culture of service that strengthens relational bonds over time. This alignment of family vision with impact-oriented wealth strategy not only preserves assets but enriches their meaning, ensuring that financial resources serve as vehicles for empowering others, sustaining traditions, and adapting to changing social landscapes. By embedding philanthropy into estate planning and governance structures, families inscribe a narrative of intentionality and ethical commitment, echoing themes of purpose and legacy that lie at the heart of comprehensive wealth creation.

Globally, philanthropy plays a pivotal role in addressing complex challenges such as poverty, healthcare disparities, environmental degradation, and social injustice. Wealth creators who embrace this role as active, engaged participants in the global ecosystem contribute to a collective momentum for transformative change. Such engagement transcends transactional charity, embodying solidarity and shared responsibility that honor the interconnectedness of humanity. The impact of this vision is both immediate and long-term: immediate in alleviating urgent needs, and long-term in catalyzing systemic shifts toward equity and sustainability. Incorporating this global consciousness within personal wealth strategies amplifies the potential for meaningful impact, situating individual success within the broader human story.

The psychological and social benefits of giving back also bear exploration, revealing how generosity weaves itself into the fabric of personal well-being. Studies have consistently shown that acts of giving correlate with increased happiness, reduced stress, longer lifespan, and stronger social connections. The neurochemical responses triggered by generosity—such as the release of dopamine and oxytocin—serve as internal rewards, reinforcing benevolent behavior. This biological feedback loops subtly but powerfully encourages ongoing participation in philanthropic acts, creating a cycle of reinforcement that benefits both giver and receiver. Recognizing this symbiosis offers a compelling argument for embedding generosity as an intrinsic element of wealth strategy—one that bolsters not just external circumstances but internal flourishing.

Integrating philanthropy into a broader wealth equation also introduces complexity around balancing self-interest and altruism. This dynamic tension requires humility and discernment, encouraging wealth creators to confront their deepest motivations and biases. The most impactful giving arises not from obligation or external pressure but from authentic commitment grounded in empathy and informed by reflection. Thoughtful engagement with philanthropy demands active listening to communities served, rigorous evaluation of initiatives, and openness to adapt based on evidence and feedback. This mindful approach elevates philanthropy beyond perfunctory acts to strategic investments in human and social capital, embodying the sophisticated decision-making promoted throughout the book.

Ultimately, philanthropy and giving back transcend financial calculations to become a profound statement about identity, values, and the kind of world one wishes to co-create. It challenges the notion that wealth is inherently isolating, proposing instead that it can be a deeply connective bridge between personal intention and collective well-being. Through this lens, giving back is not merely transactional but transformational, shaping the contours of who we are as individuals and as members of a global community. It inspires a vision of success that is multidimensional, intergenerational, and imbued with grace, humility, and hope.

Incorporating generosity into wealth strategy also encourages innovation in how resources are mobilized and deployed. From novel philanthropic vehicles such as impact investing and donor-advised funds to collaborations across sectors that leverage complementary strengths, the act of giving becomes a creative, dynamic endeavor. Wealth creators who adopt this mindset contribute to the evolution of the philanthropic landscape, embracing agility, experimentation, and inclusivity. This spirit resonates with the book's broader themes of adaptability and lifelong learning, underscoring that wealth in the modern era is not static but perpetually evolving mosaic shaped by intentionality, interconnectedness, and vision.

Moreover, philanthropy's role in cultivating leadership cannot be understated. Through giving, individuals often develop a heightened sense of responsibility, strategic thinking, and empathy that transcends personal benefit. Leadership in philanthropy involves fostering partnerships, inspiring others, and stewarding resources with wisdom and foresight. These qualities reinforce those needed in entrepreneurship, business, and career growth, creating reciprocal enrichment between wealth-building endeavors and acts of giving. By embracing philanthropy as both an expression and catalyst of leadership, wealth creators contribute to ecosystems of empowerment and transformation that ripple far beyond financial domains.

A final reflection considers the profound paradox of philanthropy: that in giving, one often receives far more—whether in personal fulfillment, social connection, or a generative legacy. This paradox reveals wealth's true elasticity, its capacity to expand infinitely through acts of generosity rather than dwindle through sharing. In this understanding, philanthropy becomes the very lifeblood of sustainable wealth, ensuring that it is not only amassed but diffused in ways that honor dignity, potential, and shared humanity. Embracing this truth invites every reader to reimagine their relationship with money and success, encouraging a wealthy journey that is as rich in spirit as it is in substance. In doing so, philanthropy emerges not as an afterthought but as the heart—the pulse—of enduring and ethical prosperity.

Chapter 29:
Creating a Legacy

"What you leave behind is not what is engraved in stone monuments, but what is woven into the lives of others." — Pericles

Key Takeaways

- Legacy extends beyond financial assets.
- Character is your greatest inheritance.
- Teach financial wisdom to future generations.
- Plan your estate responsibly.
- Build institutions, not just income.
- Long-term thinking creates lasting influence.
- Your legacy reflects the life you lived.

In the grand tapestry of wealth creation, the thread that truly weaves durability and significance is legacy. Legacy extends far beyond the sterile numbers in an account or the material assets passed down; it lives in the values, the wisdom, the opportunities, and the enduring impact one leaves for future generations and communities. To create a legacy that resonates through time requires envisioning wealth not just as an endpoint, but as a dynamic force that shapes lives and uplifts spirits long after the original architect is gone. Planning for such a legacy begins with embracing purpose and meaning at the core of financial ambitions, recognizing that the true power of wealth lies in its ability to serve something greater than oneself.

Purpose-driven wealth creation is transformative. When wealth is infused with meaning, it generates an intrinsic motivation that surpasses superficial gains or instant gratification. This powerful motivation is the kind that sustains disciplined effort, cultivates resilience in the face of setbacks, and invites strategic thinking that prioritizes long-term impact. Those who understand that their financial pursuits are to fuel a vision—whether to break cycles of poverty, empower communities, support education, champion innovation, or preserve the environment—are far more likely to approach wealth-building with a balance of ambition and humility. This balance nurtures ethical decisions and guards against the corrosive temptations of greed and shortsightedness. Ethical wealth creation is no mere idealistic notion; it is a practical foundation for durability, since wealth gained and preserved without integrity is inherently fragile and prone to erosion.

Creating a legacy is, therefore, an exercise in responsible stewardship. It demands that each step in the journey from earning to investing to spending and giving be interconnected, deliberate, and aligned with one's deepest values. This kind of stewardship transforms wealth from a private treasure into a shared resource that elevates not only the immediate family but also communities and, by extension, society. Wealth becomes a vehicle for opportunity creation, enabling access to quality education, healthcare, entrepreneurship, cultural enrichment, and social mobility. In this sense, a legacy is not about the amount of money transferred but about the qualitative change that the transfer enables change reflected in enriched lives, expanded horizons, and strengthened social fabric.

Moreover, legacy is about storytelling and cultural transmission. The stories and principles communicated alongside inherited assets shape the behaviors and attitudes of successors. When families cultivate traditions of generosity, innovation, discipline, and lifelong learning, they build a lineage of empowered individuals who carry forward the vision and values of previous generations. They transform the abstract concept of wealth into a living, evolving heritage that adapts to new realities but remains true to its essence. By instilling a sense of ownership and purpose in heirs, legacy also forestalls the all-too-common narratives of inherited wealth dissipating over time due to lack of preparedness or motivation.

The intertwining of legacy with leadership cannot be overstated. True wealth creators recognize that their influence must extend beyond their immediate business or professional achievements. They seek mentor, champion causes, and contribute expertise to solve complex social and economic challenges. This leadership reinforces the impact of tangible wealth by inspiring others to pursue their potential, enabling a multiplying effect on collective prosperity. As wealth accumulates, so does the potential for societal transformation, but only if wielded with vision and care.

In this context, philanthropy is not just a final act of giving but an integral part of the wealth-building process. Strategic philanthropy channels resources toward sustainable initiatives that empower recipients rather than imposing dependency. Whether supporting educational scholarships, technological innovation, social entrepreneurship, or environmental restoration, philanthropic efforts embedded in the legacy vision multiply wealth's positive impact exponentially. The power of giving also models an important lesson: that wealth is a tool to be wielded consciously, not merely hoarded or enjoyed in isolation.

Importantly, crafting a legacy necessitates vulnerability and reflection, prompting individuals to confront their mortality and the impermanence of material success. This confrontation is not morbid but motivating, urging a shift from accumulation to contribution. It demands intentional planning, legal, financial, and relational—to translate vague aspirations into concrete frameworks that endure. Estate planning, trusts, foundations, family governance structures, and educational programs can all serve as pillars supporting a sustainable legacy. These tools ensure that wealth supports generational empowerment and community enrichment rather than dissipating due to conflict, mismanagement, or neglect.

The legacy mindset also challenges contemporary fixations on individualism and immediate results. Instead, it cultivates patience and a horizon that stretches beyond a single lifetime. It invites reflection on what kind of world one wishes to inhabit—or help create—decades and centuries hence. This vision motivates a broader embrace of sustainability, equity, and innovation as pillars of wealth preservation and growth. Meaningful legacy, then, aligns personal prosperity with planetary and societal well-being, transforming private success into a public good.

The power of technology, particularly artificial intelligence and data analytics, offers new possibilities for legacy creation. These tools enable more sophisticated planning, impact measurement, and resource allocation, helping wealth creators optimize their efforts and adapt strategies over time. Emerging platforms also facilitate transparent and inclusive philanthropy, as well as mentorship programs that reach beyond geographic and socio-economic boundaries. Harnessing these advances connects legacy-minded individuals with global networks and resources, amplifying their ability to create enduring change.

However, the essence of legacy remains grounded in human values and connections. It requires nurturing relationships characterized by trust, love, education, and mutual support. Legacy is ultimately relational: the impact one has on others' lives and the values passed down through generations constitute the most profound form of wealth. As wealth ignites opportunities, the quality of relationships acts as a catalyst for turning potential into lived reality. Families and communities that gather around shared visions and ethical practices generate environments where both financial and personal growth thrive in harmony.

In sum, creating a legacy invites us to redefine wealth from a finite possession into a perpetual system of value transfer. It challenges us to think expansively about the kinds of wealth that endure psychological, social, intellectual, and moral wealth. By embedding purpose, discipline, ethics, and strategic planning into our wealth-building journey, we can construct legacies that do more than sustain material riches—they inspire new generations to dream bigger, act wiser, and live fuller lives. This holistic approach to legacy honors the interconnectedness of people, purpose, and prosperity, ultimately transforming wealth into an instrument for lasting good.

Legacy frames wealth within the immensity of time and human experience, calling each of us to steward our resources not merely for individual comfort but for the flourishing of communities and future dreamers. It reminds us that the most valuable inheritance is not the sum in a bank account, but the enduring belief that intentional, compassionate, and wise stewardship of wealth can elevate humanity. This belief, when put into practice, becomes a beacon—a source of motivation, a foundation for ethical wealth creation, and a means to unleash a ripple effect of positive impact that transcends generations. Through this lens, the creation of legacy becomes the ultimate expression of financial freedom and success: wealth not accumulated for its own sake, but wealth used as a powerful, purposeful force for meaningful transformation into the future.

Chapter 30: Synthesizing The Wealth Equation

"Success is neither magical nor mysterious. Success is the natural consequence of consistently applying basic fundamentals." — Jim Rohn

Key Takeaways

- Wealth is built through mindset, knowledge, and action.
- Skills multiply earning potential.
- Strategic investing accelerates financial growth.
- Relationships create opportunities.
- Technology expands wealth-building possibilities.
- Discipline sustains long-term success.
- Purpose transforms wealth into lasting significance.

Integrating Skills, Strategy, and Technology

Wealth creation in the modern era transcends traditional boundaries, demanding an integration of skills, strategy, and technology in a dynamic and harmonious collision that generates results far greater than the sum of individual efforts. At the heart of this synthesis lies a profound understanding: knowledge is multifaceted, and isolated mastery in one domain is rarely sufficient to propel an individual into sustained financial freedom. Instead, it is the deliberate weaving together of varied disciplines—the nuanced mastery of skills that refine personal and professional capabilities, the careful crafting and execution of strategy that aligns actions with long-term visions, and the innovative adoption of technology that amplifies reach and efficiency—that unlocks the true potential for lasting wealth. This integration represents not merely a checklist of competencies but a transformative paradigm shift, requiring both introspective awareness and outward adaptability.

Consider an entrepreneur standing at the nexus of these three pillars. They might possess exceptional skills in product development, harnessing a deep understanding of market needs and customer psychology. Yet, without a strategic framework to identify opportunities, allocate resources, and mitigate risks, their efforts risk drifting aimlessly against a turbulent marketplace. Layer in technology—perhaps artificial intelligence tools that analyze consumer behavior, automate mundane tasks, and provide predictive insights—and suddenly, the entrepreneur transcends conventional constraints, crafting offerings tailored with surgical precision and operating with an efficiency previously inconceivable. This synergy is not an accident but the result of intentional and continuous integration, a deliberate process that ensures each element enhances, complements, and elevates the others.

The foundational principle at play here is that skills, strategy, and technology are mutually reinforcing components of a holistic wealth-building system. Skills represent the human capital—the acquired competencies and talents that shape our approach to problems and opportunities. Strategy acts as guiding intelligence, the mental architecture that determines priorities, sequences actions, and manages complexity. Technology serves as an amplifier, extending reach, accelerating processes, and enabling innovative approaches that disrupt traditional models. To separate these elements is to forgo the exponential gains that come from their fusion. Instead, a deliberate commitment to blend these forces propels individuals beyond piecemeal success toward the fertile ground of financial independence and growth.

To operationalize this vision, readers must first engage deeply in self-assessment, aligning their innate strengths and acquired skills with an evolving strategic framework and a clear-eyed embrace of appropriate technological tools. This begins with cultivating a diverse skill set that is both adaptable and specialized. In the realm of career development, for example, this might mean combining hard technical expertise with soft skills such as communication, negotiation, and emotional intelligence. The workplace and market landscape are increasingly fluid, and those who succeed are often those who can pivot seamlessly, learning new competencies while deepening existing ones. The cultivation of leadership skills further amplifies this capacity, enabling individuals not only to direct their own trajectories but to inspire and mobilize others, creating ecosystems of opportunity that extend beyond solitary endeavors.

Strategy, by contrast, requires a broader advantage. It demands that individuals look beyond immediate gains to comprehend systemic forces, market patterns, and emergent trends. To build a robust wealth strategy, one must integrate short-term tactics with long-term visions. This includes understanding risk management, capital allocation, market timing, and diversification principles, but also involves more intangible elements such as aligning financial goals with personal values and life purpose. A strategy divorced from authentic purpose risks generating wealth that is hollow or unsustainable, while a strategy rooted in clarity of intention serves as an unshakable compass that keeps decisions anchored even amid volatility. Strategic thinking also compels continuous learning—not as an abstract ideal but as an applied discipline requiring rigorous analysis, scenario planning, and reflective adaptation.

Technology's role cannot be overstated in this constellation. The rapid acceleration of innovation, particularly in artificial intelligence, data analytics, and digital platforms, has democratized access to powerful tools once reserved for elite institutions. These technologies, when harnessed wisely, furnish individuals with unprecedented capabilities: real-time data to inform investment decisions, automation to streamline business operations, and connectivity to access global marketplaces and communities. But technology is a double-edged sword; it demands not only savvy adoption but also critical discernment. Blind reliance on tools without a foundational skill set or strategic rationale can lead to overconfidence, resource misallocation, or ethical pitfalls. Thus, technology must be integrated as an enabler within a broader architecture of skills and strategy, rather than as a standalone panacea.

The practical pathway toward this integration starts with deliberate education and training, not only in technical proficiencies but also in cognitive frameworks that support strategic thinking and technological literacy. Courses, coaching, and real-world experience all play pivotal roles, but so too do reflective practices such as journaling, mentorship, and peer collaboration. These endeavors cultivate a mindset primed for synthesis—a capacity to connect dots, identify patterns, and make decisions amid ambiguity. Moreover, engagement with diverse perspectives broadens one's cognitive toolkit, fostering innovation and resilience. For instance, navigating complex financial landscapes demands fluency in economics, psychology, and emerging digital paradigms, all of which can be cultivated through interdisciplinary learning.

Another critical element is the conscious design of personalized wealth-building plans that balance ambition with realism, flexibility with discipline. Such plans must articulate clear goals but remain adaptable to shifting circumstances and technological disruptions. They incorporate measurable milestones and feedback loops that allow for course correction, leveraging both quantitative metrics and qualitative insights. Building this adaptability is itself a skill—a meta-competence that undergirds sustained success. It enables individuals to seize emergent opportunities enabled by technological advances while managing risks inherent in innovation-driven markets.

Importantly, the integration process is deeply relational and contextual. Relationships form the social fabric in which skills, strategy, and technology manifest their impact. Networking, partnerships, and communities of practice create supportive environments that foster knowledge exchange, opportunities, and accountability. These relational ties are not mere conveniences but strategic assets that amplify efforts and open doors that remain closed to isolated individuals. Collaborative ventures can multiply creativity and resource mobilization, while social feedback sharpens judgment and expands horizons. In this light, relationship-building assumes strategic importance, encouraged and nurtured alongside personal development and technological sophistication.

As readers bring these insights into their lives, it's essential to embrace a mindset of stewardship—recognizing that wealth is a tool for service as much as a marker of personal achievement. This perspective aligns financial aspirations with broader contributions to family, community, and society. When skills, strategy, and technology are wielded ethically and purposefully, they become instruments for generating not only economic abundance but also social value. This deepens the meaning and sustainability of wealth, embedding it in wisdom, character, and legacy. The process of integration thus becomes transformative, elevating wealth creation from transactional to transcendental.

Inspiration for this journey can be found in countless real-world examples—visionary leaders who have combined acumen, insight, and innovation to disrupt traditional industries and build empires grounded in principled leadership. Their stories illuminate the power of integrative thinking and demonstrate that the path to financial freedom is neither smooth nor linear but profoundly rewarding when pursued with disciplined passion and resilience. These narratives serve not only as motivation but as blueprints for action, illustrating how setbacks can become pivots, complexity can breed creativity, and technology can magnify human potential.

Practical implementation is further supported by exercises that invite active participation: envisioning personal wealth equations that define unique value propositions and resources; mapping strategic priorities aligned with core values; identifying technological tools that complement individual strengths and aspirations; and designing feedback mechanisms that foster continuous improvement. This active engagement transforms passive reading into dynamic growth, fostering ownership and accountability that are essential for long-term change. By embedding these practices in daily routines, readers cultivate habits that anchor their wealth-building journey within evolving realities.

Ultimately, integrating skills, strategy, and technology is more than a theoretical ideal; it is the authentic pathway toward financial freedom in an increasingly complex and interconnected world. The fusion of these elements creates adaptive, resilient, and innovative individuals capable of navigating uncertainty with confidence and purpose. It empowers them to transform knowledge into action, challenges into opportunities, and assets into legacies. This integration honors the full spectrum of human potential—intellectual, strategic, technological, and ethical—offering a compelling blueprint for those who dare to build wealth not only as an end but as a means toward a fulfilling and impactful life. Embracing this integrative approach, readers embark on a lifelong journey marked by growth, discovery, and the realization of dreams that resonate far beyond mere dollars and cents.

Chapter 31: Creating Your Wealth Plan

"A goal without a plan is just a wish." — *Antoine de Saint-Exupéry*

Key Takeaways

- Every financial journey requires a written plan.
- Set clear, measurable financial goals.
- Track progress regularly.
- Review and update your plan annually.
- Align spending with priorities.
- Commit to disciplined execution.
- Success follows intentional planning.

Crafting a personalized wealth plan is more than a financial exercise; it is an act of self-discovery, intention, and empowerment that aligns your financial aspirations with your values, skills, and life purpose. The journey to financial freedom begins not with numbers alone, but with clarity around what wealth means uniquely to you, the deep motivations driving your pursuit, and the realistic yet ambitious roadmap you outline to turn vision into vibrant reality.

Embarking on this path involves embracing both the art and science of money management—a blend of disciplined strategy, mindful reflection, and adaptive foresight. The process begins with a foundational step: defining your vision of wealth. This is where you take pause and reflect honestly on the kinds of freedoms and opportunities you want your financial resources to unlock. Do you envision a life free from the stress of monthly bills, allowing you to focus on creative passions? Is your ambition to build a legacy that supports your family and empowers future generations? Or perhaps it is the aspiration to create societal impact through philanthropy or entrepreneurial ventures. Crafting a wealth plan forces you to move beyond vague notions of success and surface an intimate portrait of what a richly fulfilling life truly looks like. It calls for exercises in visualization, journaling, and dialog with trusted mentors or peers, all aimed at crystallizing your financial purpose into tangible goals. Once the vision is clear, the next crucial phase is assessment: taking stock of your current financial reality with uncompromising honesty and detail. This means diving into your income streams, expenses, debts, savings, investments, and even intangible assets like skills and networks. It is often a moment of awakening, where the abstract concept of "wealth" becomes quantified and contextualized within the framework of your everyday existence. Without this transparent inventory, any plan risks being detached from feasibility or tailored support.

The goal here is not judgment but empowerment—a clear-eyed understanding of your starting point that will guide realistic pacing and prioritization moving forward. This comprehensive self-audit also shines a light on recurring patterns and psychological blockages related to money, which may have subtly undermined past efforts. Recognizing these is essential for transforming mindset and behavior alongside financial structures. Armed with clarity on both your destination and departure point, the creation of a strategic action plan unfolds naturally as the bridge between intention and impact. This entails setting measurable, time-bound goals that reflect your wealth priorities—whether it be eliminating debt, building emergency savings, investing in education, or launching a business. The power of specificity cannot be overstated here; it turns nebulous hopes into accountable commitments. Integrating key financial principles, such as living below your means, diversifying income, and automating savings, the plan becomes a practical blueprint that adapts to life's waves without losing sight of the overarching vision. Within this stage, it's critical to balance ambition with prudence and infuse flexibility into your strategy. Life is dynamic and unpredictable, and the best plans evolve in rhythm with change rather than buckle under its weight. Hence, incorporating periodic reviews and recalibrations into your process ensures resilience and keeps motivation fueled by measurable progress. One vital yet often overlooked component of crafting a wealth plan is the alignment of your financial goals with your core values and lifestyle preferences. Money, when untethered from what gives life meaning, can become an empty pursuit. By rooting your plan in the values that define you—be it independence, creativity, family, or social contribution—you transform wealth from a mere accumulation of assets into a purposeful foundation that supports the life you desire. This ethical anchoring not only inspires steadiness through challenges but cultivates a richer sense of fulfillment as achievements align authentically with who you are. Another profound element involves skill development and education mapped into your plan.

Recognizing that wealth creation is not static, but a continuum of learning and adaptability, the best strategies prioritize upgrading skills related to career advancement, financial literacy, and entrepreneurial competence. This may include scheduling time for courses, seeking mentorship, or joining communities that foster shared growth. The intentional cultivation of human capital concurrently protects and amplifies financial capital, ensuring your plan remains robust amid changing economic landscapes. Simultaneously, your wealth plan must incorporate the cultivation and maintenance of relationships as both emotional support systems and strategic assets. Trustworthy networks provide access to opportunities, knowledge, and encouragement critical to sustaining momentum. Planning regular engagement with mentors, peers, and professional advisors enhances accountability and opens pathways that may otherwise remain inaccessible. This relational dimension underscores the intrinsically social nature of wealth building—a reminder that success is rarely a solo endeavor but rather a tapestry woven through collaboration and shared insight. Integral to the operational aspects of your wealth plan is the mastering of budgeting and cash flow management. Thoughtful allocation of income to cover essential living costs, savings, investments, and discretionary spending forms the daily structure that enables long-term goals to manifest.

Developing habits such as reviewing financial statements, using technology tools for tracking, and anticipating irregular expenses ensures proactive control over resources. This ongoing mindfulness guards against impulsivity and builds confidence, reinforcing the sense that you command your financial reality rather than being at its mercy. Debt management also deserves a central place in crafting your plan. Whether it involves eliminating high-interest consumer debt or strategically leveraging credit for growth opportunities, clear objectives and timelines for repayment reduce burden and open space for saving and investing.

Approaching debt with discipline transforms it from a source of stress to a tactical instrument employed judiciously, reflecting a mature understanding of leverage and risk. Another transformative dimension in personal wealth planning is incorporating investment strategies aligned with your risk tolerance, timeline, and ethical considerations. Far beyond simply parking money, investing is about fueling growth and diversity that unlocks multiple streams of income. Your plan should articulate your comfort with different asset classes—stocks, bonds, real estate, entrepreneurship, or alternative investments—and set incremental targets for portfolio diversification. Informed by continuous education and professional advice, this facet of your strategy enhances compound growth and financial security, lightening dependency on a single income source. Alongside traditional investment, weaving technology and innovation into your plan significantly elevates potential and efficiency. Harnessing digital tools for budgeting, trading, and financial education not only saves time but increases precision and adaptability. Importantly, staying abreast of emerging trends such as artificial intelligence in asset management or automated wealth platforms fosters a future-forward mindset. Integrating experimentation with new technologies as a deliberate component of your plan encourages ongoing learning and positions you to capitalize on advancements that multiply your financial edge. Emotional resilience is frequently the unseen force behind the success of any wealth plan.

The highs and lows of financial journeys can elicit fear, impatience, or complacency, challenging even the most well-crafted strategies. Embedding practices of mindfulness, gratitude, and deliberate reflection within your plan buttresses mental and emotional well-being, equipping you to pivot gracefully in the face of setbacks. Cultivating a narrative of patience and abundance reframes obstacles as lessons and progress as incremental victories, sustaining your motivation across seasons. A powerful catalyst in personalizing your wealth plan is storytelling—crafting your financial narrative that honors past experiences, celebrates present achievements, and envisions future triumphs. This evolving story acts as a compass, clarifying priorities and fostering ownership over the journey.

Sharing your narrative with trusted confidents not only deepens connection but invites accountability and encouragement, turning abstract goals into shared commitments. This human element infuses your plan with vitality and depth beyond numbers alone. Practical implementation is the final and most critical step in creating a wealth plan, transforming ideas into habitual actions. Establishing routines, such as monthly financial reviews or quarterly goal assessments, provides structure and momentum. Using visual tools like vision boards, progress charts, or digital dashboards keeps focus sharp and progress tangible. Incorporating reminders and rewards for milestones creates positive reinforcement loops, making wealth building a gratifying process rather than a daunting chore. Importantly, remaining open to feedback and learning from setbacks fosters a growth mindset, ensuring the plan evolves dynamically rather than becoming rigid or discouraging.

The transformational power of a personalized wealth plan is best appreciated in its ability to integrate all these elements—vision clarity, realistic assessment, strategic goal setting, value alignment, skill cultivation, relationship building, disciplined money management, leveraged investing, technology adoption, emotional resilience, storytelling, and practical action—into a coherent, living framework that adapts as you change and grow. It is a testament to the truth that wealth is not a destination but an ongoing equation, solved uniquely by everyone through dedication, wisdom, and purposeful choices. As you embark on creating your own wealth plan, remember that perfection is not the goal; progress and intentionality are. The plan is your compass, your mentor, and your mirror, reflecting both where you aspire to go and who you are becoming. Keep it alive, keep it aligned with your deepest desires and values, and allow it to inspire you not just towards financial freedom, but towards a flourishing, meaningful life. This is your invitation to shift from passive money management into active wealth creation, transforming financial hope into a legacy that honors your vision, your discipline, and your limitless potential.

Chapter 32: Sustaining Growth and Adaptation

"It is not the strongest of the species that survive, nor the most intelligent, but the one most responsive to change." — Commonly attributed to Charles Darwin

Key Takeaways

- Wealth creation is a lifelong journey.
- Continue learning as markets evolve.
- Adapt to changing technologies and economies.
- Review strategies regularly.
- Stay resilient during uncertainty.
- Never stop investing in yourself.
- Sustainable wealth is built through continuous growth, ethical leadership, and purposeful action.

The journey to wealth is not a sprint but a marathon, demanding not only an initial burst of energy but a sustained, ongoing commitment to growth and adaptation. Maintaining momentum over the long haul requires a delicate balance of discipline, flexibility, and continual learning. It is a dance between steadfast conviction in your goals and the agility to pivot when circumstances, markets, and personal situations evolve. The truth is that wealth built without constant care and adjustment tends to erode. Just as a gardener cannot plant a seed and expect a flourishing garden without tending to it, individuals must nurture their wealth-building processes regularly and thoughtfully. This ongoing engagement is the bedrock of sustaining growth and adapting to change, ensuring that financial freedom is not just achieved but preserved and amplified over time.

One of the foundational principles of sustaining growth is recognizing that change is the only constant. Economic environments shift, technologies emerge and disrupt, industries transform, and even personal lives evolve in unforeseen ways. With this reality firmly understood, the first step to maintaining momentum is embracing a mindset of perpetual adaptability. Instead of resisting change or clinging stubbornly to old plans, successful wealth creators cultivate curiosity and openness. They treat shifts not as threats but as opportunities to innovate and refine their strategies. This proactive stance toward change prevents stagnation, enabling individuals to remain relevant and resilient in a world where static approaches frequently lead to obsolescence. Practically, this means keeping one's ear to the ground—absorbing trends, seeking new knowledge, and remaining connected with thought leaders and peers who can provide insights and alternative perspectives.

In tandem with mindset, discipline anchors growth. The excitement that fuels initial wealth-building endeavors is often intoxicating, yet as time wears on, it is discipline—consistent habits, repeated behaviors, and accountability to oneself—that carries the weight. Discipline shapes everyday actions, ensuring that deliberate steps are taken regularly, no matter how small, toward the overarching financial vision. This ethic protects against distractions and temptations that otherwise erode progress, whether it's an impulsive purchase, neglecting continued education, or ignoring the necessary reviews of one's portfolio or business operations. Sustaining this discipline requires creating systems and routines that support desired behaviors. Whether it's a dedicated weekly review of finances, regularly scheduled skill-building sessions, or periodic reflection on goals, embedding structure within the journey serves as a compass to keep the course steady, even amid periodical doubt or external pressures.

However, discipline alone without reflection is not enough to sustain growth. Another key principle is the importance of feedback loops and regular self-assessment. Wealth-building is a dynamic process, and continual evaluation uncovers blind spots, recognizes obstacles early, and reveals untapped opportunities. By systematically analyzing results, behaviors, and environments, individuals learn what strategies yield returns and which ones need modification. This reflective practice can take many forms: journaling financial outcomes, engaging coaches or mentors, participating in mastermind groups, or leveraging data analytics tools enabled by modern technology. Harnessing these mechanisms not only deepens self-awareness but builds the confidence to pivot where necessary with informed intent rather than reactive emotion. It nurtures a learning orientation that transforms setbacks into springboards, turning failures into invaluable lessons rather than defeats.

Accompanying self-assessment is the imperative for lifelong learning—a principle tightly woven into the fabric of adaptation. The rapid pace of change in today's global economy demands that wealth creators continuously expand their knowledge and skills. This extends beyond financial literacy alone to encompass new technologies, leadership methods, entrepreneurial innovations, and even emotional intelligence. A commitment to lifelong learning expands capacity, sharpens strategic thinking, and keeps one prepared to capitalize on emerging assets and opportunities. Practically, this may mean formal education such as courses and certifications, informal study such as reading and podcasts, or experiential learning through new ventures and collaborations. Importantly, learning is not solely about accumulation of facts but about developing the ability to connect disparate ideas and apply insights creatively. It fosters mental flexibility, enhances problem-solving, and fuels innovation in the face of complex, evolving market forces.

Maintaining momentum also involves the thoughtful management of resources across multiple dimensions. Financial capital, human capital, and time are all finite and demand stewardship that maximizes their utility. Diversification of income streams, for example, reduces vulnerability and encourages growth by spreading risk. Simultaneously, investing in relationships and networks cultivates social capital that opens doors, generates ideas, and provides support during difficult phases. Time management practices ensure that focus remains on high-value activities aligned with one's purpose and goals. Recognizing the interplay among these resources empowers individuals to allocate attention and effort where they best of the growth, rather than dissipating energy on distractions or reactive firefighting.

Technology, especially artificial intelligence, emerges as a crucial enabler in sustaining growth and adaptation. It offers tools that streamline decision-making, provide deep analysis, and automate mundane tasks, freeing mental space for strategic thinking. For instance, AI-driven financial advisors can monitor markets and portfolios continuously, alerting them to opportunities or risks faster than traditional methods. Similarly, AI-powered learning platforms personalize education, helping learners acquire new skills more efficiently. Adopting such technologies is less about fetishizing gadgets and more about integrating intelligent systems that augment human capabilities. Yet, this requires a mindset open to experimentation and cautious governance to ensure ethical and purposeful use. Leveraging technology skillfully accelerates progress while mitigating human limitations, making it an indispensable asset for sustained wealth building.

Yet beyond systems, disciplines, and technologies, sustaining growth ultimately rests on cultivating an inner alignment—clarity of purpose and values that act as an internal compass through changing circumstances. Without a deeply held sense of why wealth matters and for whom it is built, the pursuit easily devolves into empty accumulation or misguided risk-taking. Purpose fuels resilience when setbacks arise, guiding focus toward meaningful long-term goals rather than transient gains. It shapes choices about what financial pursuits, relationships, and philosophies resonate authentically, avoiding scattershot efforts that drain energy. This alignment also encourages stewardship over legacy, encouraging individuals to consider how their wealth impacts communities and future generations. In this sense, money becomes more than a means—it becomes a vehicle for purpose-driven influence and enduring contribution.

In practical terms, implementing a personalized wealth-building plan that thrives through growth and adaptation starts with crafting a roadmap that integrates these principles. This plan is more than a static document; it is a living strategy subject to continuous refinement. Begin by articulating clear, meaningful financial and personal goals, embedding purpose into every intention. Follow this with a realistic assessment of current assets, skills, and resources, establishing baseline metrics. Design a framework of actions supported by routines that balance discipline with flexibility. Schedule regular checkpoints to reflect and recalibrate, inviting feedback and external perspectives. Prioritize ongoing education and network cultivation with dedicated time and energy, embedding learning as a core value. Explore and incorporate appropriate technologies thoughtfully, aligning them with your unique circumstances and ethical standards.

Perhaps the most powerful catalyst for sustained growth is embracing the rich interplay between action and iteration. Wealth creation is not about perfection but about taking consistent, informed steps forward while actively learning and adapting. Each success provides confidence; each challenge offers insight; every adjustment sharpens your trajectory. This mindset dismantles paralysis born of fear or overwhelm and replaces it with empowered momentum. Recognize that sustaining wealth over decades means welcoming evolution in both the external environment and within yourself. What worked yesterday may falter tomorrow, and that is not failure but a call to innovate and improve. Sustained growth is therefore a dynamic process—an ever-unfolding story of intentional progress interwoven with resilience and learned wisdom.

Inspiring yourself to embark on this lifelong journey requires cultivating patience and a long view of wealth—not measured merely by bank balances but by freedom, security, the ability to contribute meaningfully, and the legacy left behind. Remember that millions of individuals who have attained lasting financial freedom share one common thread: they committed not just to building wealth but to maintaining and adapting it through life's inevitable uncertainties. Your personalized plan, guided by the principles of mindset, discipline, reflection, learning, resource management, technology adoption, and purpose will empower you to do the same.

As you proceed beyond this chapter, carry forward the understanding that the wealth equation is not a closed formula but a living equation. It changes with values, circumstances, and ambitions, requiring constant recalibration. Yet within its fluidity lies immense potential—the possibility for you, the dreamer and doer, to sustain growth that empowers a life of freedom, fulfillment, and impact. You are called not merely to build wealth but to steward it, to steward yourself, and to steward a legacy that transcends generations. This ongoing commitment to growth and adaptation transforms wealth creation from an event into an enduring way of being. Let this understanding infuse each day with purpose, motivation, and the courageous resolve to keep moving forward, no matter what challenges arise. With every step taken, you write the story of your financial future—one that is as resilient and vibrant as the vision that inspires you.

Reader Reflection

Reflection Questions

As you complete this book, consider the following:

- What limiting beliefs about money have you overcome?
- Which financial habit has had the greatest impact on your life?
- How has your definition of wealth changed?
- What new income opportunities will you pursue?
- How will you use wealth to serve others?
- What legacy do you want your financial decisions to create?

Final Thoughts

Your Wealth Journey Begins Now

Financial freedom is not reserved for a privileged few. It belongs to those who choose to learn continuously, think strategically, act consistently, and persevere through challenges.

Every successful investor, entrepreneur, executive, and business owner began with a decision to improve their financial knowledge. The greatest investment you will ever make is in yourself.

- Your skills determine your income.
- Your habits determine your wealth.
- Your character determines your legacy.

The future you desire begins with the decisions you make today. May this book inspire you to take those decisions with confidence.

Companion Resources: Your Personal Wealth Toolkit

A practical workbook to accompany *The Wealth Equation*.

1. Personal Wealth Planner

Define your mission, vision and long-term goals.

Section	**Your Response**
Personal Mission Statement	
Financial Vision	
Five-Year Goals	
Ten-Year Goals	
Retirement Goals	

Section	Your Response
Legacy Goals	

2. Monthly Budget Planner

Track income and expenses monthly.

Category	Amount	Notes
Salary		
Business Income		
Investments		
Other Income		
Housing		
Transportation		
Utilities		
Food		

Category	**Amount**	**Notes**
Insurance		
Debt Payments		
Entertainment		
Savings		
Investments		
Net Cash Flow		

3. Net Worth Calculator

Review quarterly.

Assets	**Value**	**Liabilities**	**Value**
Cash			
Savings			
Investments			

Assets	Value	Liabilities	Value
Real Estate			
Business Ownership			
Retirement Accounts			

4. Debt Elimination Tracker

Update monthly.

Creditor	Balance	Interest %	Monthly Payment	Target Date	Remaining

5. Investment Portfolio Tracker

Monitor diversification.

Investment	Purchase Date	Purchase Price	Current Value	Annual Return %	Allocation %

6. Multiple Income Planner

Evaluate additional income.

Income Source	**Start up Cost**	**Expected Monthly Income**	**Risk**	**Implementation Date**	**Status**

7. Skills Investment Plan

Invest in yourself.

Current Skill	Desired Skill	Training	Cost	Expected Salary Increase	Completion

8. Entrepreneurship Canvas

Plan before launching.

Business Element	**Details**
Business Idea	
Target Customer	
Value Proposition	
Revenue Sources	
Estimated Startup Cost	
Marketing Strategy	
Growth Plan	

9. Annual Wealth Review

Reflect annually.

Question	Response
How much did my net worth increase?	
How much did I save?	
How much did I invest?	
What financial mistakes did I make?	
What lessons did I learn?	
What will I improve next year?	

10. Twelve-Month Financial Action Plan

Month	Milestone	Completed?
January	Financial assessment and goal setting.	☐
February	Create or revise a monthly budget.	☐
March	Build or strengthen your emergency fund.	☐
April	Increase retirement contributions.	☐
May	Develop a new professional skill.	☐
June	Launch or expand a side business.	☐
July	Review investment performance.	☐
August	Reduce unnecessary expenses.	☐

Month	Milestone	Completed?
September	Increase passive income.	□
October	Review insurance and risk protection.	□
November	Update estate and legacy plans.	□
December	Conduct an annual financial review and prepare goals for the coming year.	□

Suggested Wealth-Building Workflow

Financial Vision → Annual Goals → Monthly Budget → Savings & Investing

↓

Quarterly Review → Adjust Strategy → Long-Term Wealth & Legacy

Closing Message to Readers

Your Financial Journey Continues

Completing this book is not the end of your wealth-building journey, it is the beginning.

Wealth = Mindset × Skills × Strategy × Discipline × Relationships × Technology × Purpose – Poor Decision

Use this toolkit throughout the year to plan, measure, review, and improve your financial decisions. Consistent action, ethical stewardship, and continuous learning are the foundation of sustainable wealth and legacy.

Every chapter you have read represents an invitation to take action. Knowledge becomes valuable only when it is applied consistently. Financial freedom is rarely the result of a single breakthrough; it is built through disciplined decisions repeated over time.

Your income may determine where you begin, but your mindset, skills, habits, and character will determine where you finish.

Remember the central principle of this book:

Wealth = Mindset × Skills × Strategy × Discipline × Relationships × Technology × Purpose – Poor Decision

When these elements work together, financial success becomes sustainable, meaningful, and transformational.

I encourage you to revisit this book regularly, use the companion resources to track your progress, and remain committed to continuous learning and ethical stewardship. As your knowledge grows, so will your opportunities to create value, build prosperity, and leave a legacy that benefits others.

The equation is now in your hands. Solve it with wisdom, perseverance, and purpose. The future you desire begins with the decisions you make today.

Your 12-Month Wealth Action Plan

A month-by-month implementation guide.

January
    Financial assessment.
February
    Budget creation.
March
    Emergency fund.
April
    Investing.
May
    Skill development.
June
    Side business.
July
    Portfolio review.
August
    Debt reduction.
September
    Passive income.
October
    Tax planning.
November
    Estate planning.
December
    Annual review.

Other Books by the Author

- *Strategic HR Mastery: Harnessing People Power to Thrive in Tomorrow's Workplace*
- *Human Intelligence in the Age of AI*
- *Beyond the Degree: Building a Future-Proof Career in the Age of Artificial Intelligence*
- *The Governance Revolution: Why Leadership Must Change Before Society Breaks*
- *Kingdoms of Tomorrow*
- *The Harvest of Kings*
- *Reinventing Development*
- *The Audacity of Perseverance* (Coming Soon)